PETER FRAMPTON

Madison Square Garden, NYC, 1976   *Chuck Pulin*

Peter Frampton

by Irene Adler

quick fox

New York • London • Tokyo

International Standard Book Number: ISBN: 0-8256-3933-6

Library of Congress Catalog Card Number: 79-63526

Printed in the United States of America.

In Great Britain: Book Sales Ltd.,
78 Newman Street, London W1, England

In Canada: Gage Trade Publishing,
P.O. Box 5000, 164 Commander Blvd.,
Agincourt, Ontario M1S 3C7, Canada

In Japan: Music Sales Corporation,
4-26-22 Jingumae, Shibuya-Ku,
Tokyo 150, Japan

Designed by Jacques Chazaud

Front cover photography courtesy United Press International

Back cover photography by Judi Lesta

Typeset by Filmar Graphics, Inc., San Diego, CA

INTRODUCTION

Peter Frampton is different. While other stars are cold, he is overtly friendly and warm. While other stars are arrogant, he is sweet. His boyish good looks, impish grin leading to a large, open smile, and disarming sincerity have established him forever in the hearts of pop music lovers. Even his critics say that it is hard to put him down because he's such a nice guy.

Peter is like the boy next door. How else can you describe someone who claims that he and his German Shepherd Rocky talk to each other when they're alone, whose closest relationship is with his parents, and who readily admits that when the TV show *Bewitched* changed its male lead, "Darrin," that he never could accept the new "Darrin?"

Peter has made niceness a new phenomenon in the rock industry. On stage he communicates with his audiences as individuals. When he smilingly sings "my family of friends," gesturing out toward the crowd, a roar of appreciation wafts out and back toward Peter. Indeed his audience, which for the past five years Peter has nurtured and developed from a small following to a large crowd to the worldwide movement it is now, is his "family of friends;" and as a performer Peter's first debt of gratitude is always to them. They range from forty-year-old housewives to twelve-year-old teeny-boppers to his ever supportive parents.

There are those who've followed his career from his early days with The Herd when Peter was in his teens; those who remember him as the dynamo of Humble Pie when he was in his early twenties; and those who've just discovered this twenty-nine-year-old virtuoso guitarist.

Peter Frampton is considered by many to be the number one guitarist today, and by most to be among the top five guitarists. This has been his earliest dream. When other little boys were envisioning themselves as future firemen or cowboys, Peter was planning on being the greatest guitarist. It is a goal toward which he has worked from the moment he picked up his first stringed-instrument — a 4-string banjulele — at age seven.

Even when Peter was with The Herd and Humble Pie, his guitar expertise was recognized. But it wasn't until 1976, when Peter released his fifth solo album, *Frampton Comes Alive!*, that his talents received the mass plaudits which catapulted him to superstardom. One writer even suggested that Peter's popularity had spread so far that the word "Frampton" should be listed as a new entry in the dictionary; as a noun signifying things which defy explanation, for example: "That's the Framptonest thing I ever saw;" and as a verb meaning a euphoric state of being, ex: "I could Frampton all day long." (*Dearborn Times Herald*, Wed. April 16, 1975)

But nobody could be more "Framptoned" by this newest wave of phenomenal success than Frampton himself. "I'm in such a daze," he says. "Do you believe all that's happening? What a giggle!"

Fortunately, Peter has had the experience of being a sought-after musician, with all the fan adoration that comes with it, twice — once with The Herd, when he was voted "Face of 1968" and again with the Pie — so he knows just how far to let success carry him. Peter's personality remains as sweet and honest as it ever was; and though he is thrilled by it all, success will bring no character changes to Peter. "I was blessed to be prepared for it," he says.

Peter has worked toward his solo recognition for nearly ten years, playing to audiences in every town and gathering his following. Both The Herd and Humble Pie were extremely popular groups, but Peter left both to go after his own style of music — melodic, jazz-influenced rock. After departing from Humble Pie, Peter was doing a lot of session work for such accomplished musicians as George Harrison, Tim Hardin, John Entwistle, and Harry Nilsson. All the while he was planning his own solo career and wondering if it would ever take off. It seemed as if Peter's soloist ambitions just wouldn't carry him. He grew more and more in debt to his faithful manager, Dee Anthony, and right up until the January, 1976, release of *Alive!* Peter considered returning to session work for good.

Happily for Peter and for his ever-growing legion of fans, that wasn't necessary. *Frampton Comes Alive!* rose steadily in the charts. That was satisfying. In one month it was in the top ten. By March it reached the number one spot where it remained for one week. In June, *Frampton Comes Alive!* regained the number one spot and held it throughout the summer and into the early fall, remaining number one for an unprecedented seventeen weeks. It became one of the supreme attractions during the extremely competitive Bicentennial summer, eventually breaking all previous records for the most number of weeks in a number one spot. The prior winner was Carole King's 1971 release *Tapestry*. What

1977 *Pictorial Parade*

9

is even more extraordinary about this feat is that *Tapestry* is a single album, while *Alive!* is a double and more expensive for the consumer. This record was broken, however, the following year by Fleetwood Mac's *Rumours*; but Peter's *Alive!* is the biggest selling double LP of all time and continues to sell at a pace which threatens to outsell "White Christmas."

With this unexpected recognition, came a new-found confidence which had been building as he toured, but which, nonetheless, was reinforced by the tremendous acceptance of his music.

His winning brand of rock, utilizing both mellow acoustic numbers and melodious electric riffs, was not embraced at first. When Peter left the Pie, known as the staunchest of boot-stomping rockers, the world wasn't overly interested in the softer, prettier sounds that Peter was making. But this was the type of music Peter had wanted to work on all along. He had been frustrated previously with the rigidity of the Pie's music. He had tired of the deafening hard rock and wanted out. He wanted to work on his own style, a style which he has made famous and which has found a wide and ever-broadening appeal.

Although at times depression made him question whether his music ever would find acceptance, Peter credits his success to the fact that he did stick it out.

Rock Music Awards, 1977   *Frank Edwards/Fotos International*

Meadowlands Stadium, NJ, 1978   *UPI*

CHILDHOOD

Peter Kenneth Frampton was born on April 22, 1950, in Beckenham, Kent, England on the outskirts of London. As can be imagined, he was a perfectly adorable baby — curly-headed with an infectious smile.

Peter's father, Owen Frampton, had worked his way through college playing guitar in dance bands and was a true jazz enthusiast, passing this love on to Peter. When Peter was born, his father was an art teacher at a local high school. His mother, when she was a teenager, had been given a scholarship to the Royal Academy of Dramatic Arts by Dame Sybil Thorndike, but had had to refuse it as she had to work to help support her family. Peter recalls that she was a frustrated actress and that she could have been a good one. Perhaps it was seeing his mother's disappointment at not having been able to pursue her career, that pushed Peter toward pursuing his own. In any event, Peter's mother has always been supportive.

Both Peter's parents sing well, and there was always music throughout the household, especially the jazz guitarists Mr. Frampton loved so well — Django Reinhardt and Stephane Grappelli. Music and love are the memories Peter took with him from his childhood. It seems evident in his pleasant disposition that his was a happy youth.

By the time Peter was past toddling he was happily plucking away on his grandmother's banjulele — sort of a cross between a banjo and a ukelele which Peter describes as "a real strange-sounding instrument. It had four strings and was tuned to a my-dog's-got-fleas tuning."

By the age of nine he had outgrown the simple instrument and begged his parents for a guitar. That Christmas, Peter received his first guitar — a steel string one — and he applied the lessons for the banjulele his father had taught him. He was playing chords for a while and his parents decided that the best thing to do would be to give him "proper" lessons and so Peter was sent to a Spanish guitar teacher. "Whenever her back was turned," he remembers, "I was playing something else. I never practiced for those lessons really that much; but it taught me how to use all the fingers on my left hand and how to pick a little."

JFK Stadium, Philadelphia, 1977 *Chuck Pulin*   Madison Square Garden, NYC, 1976 *Chuck Pulin*

His parents were pleased with his progress and encouraged him. In fact, they never really had to push him toward the guitar, but they did not prevent him from following his ambitions. Peter's desire was to reproduce the jazz sounds he had come to love. He remembers clearly just how he became familiar with these sounds. One day his father decided to buy a record player for the family, and when he brought it home he had two records with him — a Django Reinhardt album for himself and a Cliff Richards and The Shadows album for Peter. He still has that first album.

Soon after he got his first guitar, his grandmother, who had been a singer in the 20s, took him to London's Tin Pan Alley, Charing Cross Road, and he bought his first piece of sheet music. He went home that evening and worked at that piece until he had learned the entire song. It is just that sort of perseverence which characterizes the way which Peter works at his music today.

From the time he purchased his first piece of music, he became a regular customer of the local music shop, spending all of his allowance on records and sheet music. As a boy he chose to practice his guitar rather than play sports. Peter says that when he was eight and nine years old, he did nothing but play guitar from the moment he got home from school until bedtime.

His musical interests were Eddie Cochran, an American guitarist who was very popular in England; Elvis Presley; Cliff Richards and Adam Faith, both British; Little Anthony and the Imperials; and the immortal Buddy Holly. Buddy Holly's greatest hits "Peggy Sue" and "That'll Be The Day" (which was recently redone by Linda Ronstadt) took England as well as America by storm. Peter was fortunate enough to get to see Holly in concert as he toured England. Also in that audience were John Lennon and Eric Clapton. Peter was so enamored of Holly's expertise and style that he "rushed over to Woolworth's to buy a pair of horn-rimmed glasses so I would look like Buddy Holly." He laughs about it now, but at nine years old, that was serious stuff.

JFK Stadium, Philadelphia, 1977 *Chuck Pulin*

Frankie Valli *Judi Lesta*

Peter formed numerous bands with neighborhood boys, all struck by the rock era in which they lived, and he even won a prize in a Boy Scout talent contest for playing Holly's music.

Even at that early age, Peter's preference for progressive music had surfaced. The Ventures and The Shadows were his favorite instrumental groups. He admired the way they blended the pop and rock of the day with more progressive jazz. These were the musical facets which Peter himself always strived to integrate. In every group which he entered, a main reason for his departure was because this integration was not happening. And even now, Peter harbors a mild regret that he didn't pursue a career as a jazz guitarist. Today he loves George Benson, Wes Montgomery and Little Feat, a fabulous rock group who have managed to integrate a New Orleans jazz style into very progressive rock.

But at this time Peter was just a boy, and though he worked very hard toward his dreams, he still had school to contend with. Since his father was a teacher, it was especially difficult for him to neglect his studies, and though his parents were unusually lenient with both Peter and his younger brother, they insisted that he attend to his schoolwork. They wanted him to prepare for college, so that he could have a profession to fall back on, should that become necessary.

Peter went to Bromley Technical School where his father taught. There he met a number of other boys who were interested in music, and they walked around school carrying their instruments. During breaks and at lunchtime they would gather to practice the newest tunes. Among these boys were George Underwood, today a successful artist whose work also includes LP covers; and David Bowie, then a star art pupil who had at one time planned to be a commercial artist. Both boys were art students of Mr. Frampton, and together they formed a group called George and the Dragons. They were older and more experienced than Peter, but their musical involvement brought them together. They had a sort of rivalry going. At a school talent contest organized by Mr. Frampton, George and the Dragons, featuring David Jones (Bowie) on sax, was the starring act, and Peter's Little Ravens brought up the rear. Though Peter was only twelve at the time, his group was just as well received as the older Dragons, and Peter was well on his way toward the proficiency he now displays.

1974 *Chuck Pulin*

The Little Ravens were very popular in the local area, and Peter and the other members were earning enough pocket money playing at weddings, parties and dances. They were able to keep up to date in music, and to buy costumes and equipment as they needed it, but for various reasons, mostly related to being teenagers, the Little Ravens broke up in 1963.

Peter left Bromley Tech to attend a school which had a more music-oriented curriculum, and also to go to a school where his father wasn't a teacher. It had been difficult for Peter to be a student where his father was so involved in the activities of the boys. His parents wanted him to go to a music college, so this new high school would be a preparatory ground for it.

At about this time, British music came to the fore with the wild success of the Beatles. Whereas before American pop music had dominated the charts, as well as the entire scene, with the advent of the Beatles, promoters began looking for more British talent. All of the young groups began to fashion themselves after the Beatles. And Peter's new group, The Trubeats, were no exception. Wild clothes and an easy to spot presence were hallmarks for well-known bands, and all of the small-time bands followed this image. The Trubeats made their shows spectacular by doing a costume change in between the first and second sets. Peter laughs now, but he remembers how serious he felt at thirteen when they switched from Beatle-style jackets to "leopard-skin waistcoats." They were an extremely popular band. With their success, Peter was able to keep his sheet music collection growing and keep up to date on the latest musical developments.

Electronic equipment was becoming very popular and musicians needed to know more and more about it. Peter had a penchant for electronics and he and his brother used to fool around in the bathroom, which they had set up as an echo chamber, till all hours of the night. Plenty of other musicians recall early years using the bathroom as the echo chamber; John Sebastian even based a song on it.

The Trubeats didn't stay together very long, but that is usually the case with teenage bands. The members grow tired of each other, or they lose

Olivia Newton-John   Rock Music Awards, 1977   *Frank Edwards/Fotos International*

interest in the music, or various other reasons. But while this was always happening to the bands in which Peter was involved, he himself continued to progress well beyond the limitations of the other members. The Trubeats broke up within a year, and Peter was next asked to join The Preachers. They were a jazz-based band, and this in particular excited Peter. They used saxes, trumpets, organ, bass plus drums and guitar to create a more diverse sound than any of the previous bands in which Peter had been involved.

The Preachers were managed by Bill Wyman, one of the Rolling Stones, and this was indeed a very thrilling thing for a fourteen-year-old boy. Of course Peter was somewhat of a celebrity himself, and had even been invited to give guitar demonstrations at one of his hometown music stores. Still, this was just the type of break that Peter had been hoping would come along, and he probably never expected it to come along so early in his career. At fourteen, Peter Frampton found himself a professional musician and liking it!

Actually The Preachers were considered semi-professional, but Peter's first important recording session was with them. The engineer was a man by the name of Glyn Johns. After the session, Wyman was able to get The

Preachers on a popular live rock TV show called "Ready, Steady, Go." That show was unique because all of the well-known musicians of the day could be found at one time or another performing on it. Later, the Stones had their own show with the horrible title of "Ready, Steady, Stoned." The Preachers were showcased once as Bill Wyman's guests on that live rock show, too. It was a pretty exciting time for Peter.

But, he was still a school boy, and certainly playing these gigs was interfering with his concentration. He would come into classes exhausted and just barely pull himself through the day. Still, he held on, because his love for playing was too great to give it up. His parents remained lenient, but began to wonder just how far to let it go.

Eventually The Preachers met the same fate as Peter's two previously organized bands. Arguments split them, and Andy Bown, the keyboard man, formed a group of his own. He called his new group The Herd. But Peter stuck with The Preachers who still had the backing of Bill Wyman, a decided advantage. The Preachers signed a recording contract and put out two singles. They continued to experiment with jazz sounds, much to Peter's delight. Wyman decided to expand the group's versatility by adding two female singers and a repertoire which included soul and pop numbers. To complete the transformation, the name was changed to The Train. Wyman thought that this change would help to bring the group out of the slump they had fallen into, but nothing much happened.

In the meantime, Peter had been getting into the London club scene. Even though he was just a boy, and looked younger than his years, he was becoming well-known at the clubs. Rather than being considered a nuisance, he was respected for his talent, and was allowed to play a tune or two with the bands on stage. Most of the time, he would simply watch and listen, enraptured by the groups who had made it. No doubt this lifestyle also took its toll on his school work; but, still in all, Peter made grades well above passing.

Soon Bill Wyman became disenchanted with The Train, and left them. Without his support, the group was lost, and they disbanded. The Herd, however, had grown and flourished and was rather successful. At this point, Andy Bown asked Peter if he would like to join the group. It was a tough decision. He was dying to do it, but they were a professional group, and that would mean that Peter's school work would really be impossible to keep up with. As it was, he was arriving home from gigs just minutes before he had to be in school, falling asleep in classes, and just scraping by.

THE HERD

Because his parents wanted him to continue on to music college, Peter's passing the pre-college examination was very important. Now Peter was faced with a choice; either he quit school to join The Herd or continue with school, working toward college. He put it exactly that way to his father, and his father said to him, "Well, what would you like to do?" We know what Peter replied. He was so excited about joining this group and working once again with Andy Bown that there was no doubt in his mind what he wanted to do about school.

It was a strange life for a fifteen-year-old, but Peter managed to handle it — at least in the beginning. He reminded himself of a few things. First of all he wanted to be sure never to stray too far from his ideals of blending jazz and blues into his rock career. Although rock was definitely the way for a young musician to make it in the sixties, Peter hoped he would always be able to continue his practicing in the other two areas.

Secondly, he kept in mind what his grandmother had once told him, "Never believe what they say about you in the papers." Peter had to keep these words in his heart, because it wasn't too long before The Herd had become a rage with Britain's screaming teeny-boppers, and Peter himself had earned the dubious title of "Face of 68."

When Peter joined The Herd, his father negotiated a deal with their manager, Billy Gaff, assuring that Peter would receive fifteen pounds a week, regardless of what the other band members earned. This was about $37.50 a week, and "a terrific wage for me after just having left school," Peter says. "And that was fifteen pounds a week, come what may. Some weeks the other members in the group only made three pounds a week each, but I always got my fifteen. My father made the best deal ever for me. That was the only proviso he gave. But one week we worked a lot and the rest of the group got twenty-five pounds — and I got my fifteen. So karma came back to me."

Peter loved being with The Herd. They were becoming hotter and hotter and were soon playing regularly at the Marquee Club, one of the London clubs frequented by talent scouts. Peter is quick to point out that The Who

Madison Square Garden, NYC, 1975   *Chuck Pulin*

as well as The Stones started there. The Marquee was the type of place that, if your band could play there, you were very likely to find yourself with a recording contract, and that's just what Peter and his friends were after.

Sure enough, after about a year, Steve Rollins, a manager, heard them and asked them to do a few demos for one of the popular groups. This is how a number of groups get started. Well-known groups are presented with demo tapes which have been recorded by lesser-known groups. These demo tapes give the group an idea of how a song will sound, and then they can decide whether or not they are interested in it. For the smaller groups, demo tapes are a way of getting the band heard and can eventually lead to recordings of their own.

That's exactly how it happened for The Herd. They did a few demo tapes for a popular group known as Dave, Dee, Dozy, Beaky, Mick and Tich, and their producers decided to give The Herd a chance with a record of their own. The first was called "I Can Fly," and it promptly landed nose down. The producers decided to give them another shot with a more exciting song called "From the Underworld" based on an ancient Greek myth and backed by heavy orchestration. This song rose steadily up the charts, and remained a top ten hit for quite a while. Sixteen-year-old Peter was a big hit, and success, as he had always dreamed of it, was sure to follow. Now that The Herd had a hit, they were in great demand and soon made an appearance on Britain's Dick Clark type show, *Top of the Pops*.

24

From their one appearance there, The Herd was an instant success with England's young girls, and fan mail began to pour in. The Herd had all the right characteristics; they were young, attractive, and they had a special feature: Peter Frampton. He had assumed the role of the lead singer and more or less band leader and, although he wasn't very comfortable in this position, the fans adored him! Girls literally swooned over him, and Peter, always a shy boy, was faced with a new problem. He was named "Face of 68" and, although it was meant as a compliment from an adoring public, he fled from that type of designation for the next several years.

At the time, The Herd was a fun group to be involved with. They became regulars on *Top of the Pops*. "I was lip-synching to the records and being screamed at, having my clothes ripped and people cutting bits of my hair. It was like a dream," Peter remembers. "I was sixteen and I couldn't go out of my house."

It must have been a strange life for a young boy, preventing him from learning about the world as most boys his own age would, allowing him only to practice guitar and to become a better artist and performer. But there were other factors involved, too. Peter began a serious drinking habit while with The Herd. "I joke about it now, but it was getting pretty serious at the time. Between Bown and myself we'd down nineteen triple scotches a night at the Marquee Club. Maybe not that much, we could never stand up too well when we were playing."

The sort of success these boys were reaching at the ages they were was a bit much for them to handle, and drinking could have been the least of their problems. Luckily, Peter never took a liking to drugs. Certainly they must have been flowing as freely as the liquor, and at such an impressionable age, he's lucky he resisted. Still, Peter loved being with The Herd and doing that commercial music. They released an album, entitled *Looking Thru You*, which was a large hit in England, but never made it across the Atlantic until several years later, after Peter had left the group. *Looking Thru You* featured their hit single "From the Underworld." It was the success of that song which made their album do well, but they released just that one album. It included a song composed by Peter, however, and that helped to compensate for the growing frustration he was feeling at being packaged and sold as "the face." His song, "Woken Up the Blackbirds: Better Run," was not a hit, but it helped Peter feel that he was able to maintain his individuality.

More and more, Peter was feeling the loss of control of his situation. He didn't wish to be the lead man for the group, and he felt that his singing was not up to par. He was a guitarist first and foremost, and he was being

Madison Square Garden, NYC, 1976   *Chuck Pulin*

presented as a face for young girls to scream at. This displeased him greatly, and he and Andy Bown used liquor to help them face the screaming masses they were confronted with each time they made an appearance. The whole thing was getting very tiring. Peter was not able to play his guitar as he had planned; he was not growing and learning as fast as he had wanted to; he wasn't in this band as a direct means to an end; and he wasn't in it strictly to make money. He was there to progress, and, incidentally, to become known, which he admitted was nice. But mainly, he was there to grow as a guitarist.

Peter was disappointed with The Herd's departure from their more jazz-oriented beginnings to the more commercial stuff they were producing. It was fun for a while, but the fun aspect began to wear off. What stuck was a sinking disappointment with the aura created around the band, with the way in which the fans were shaping the type of music they were playing, and with the entire show he was forced to put on every time he stepped on stage. Peter was not cut out to be the lead man in the band, and he was not very happy with the attention he was getting at the expense of his musical integrity.

Also, the other boys were considered as the background for Peter's good looks. This began a controversy which never quite surfaced, but which the press played to the fullest. The other boys felt a justifiable resentment at Peter's notoriety, and Peter himself was only too aware of this. He was embarrassed at the attention paid his looks and began a long battle to overcome his natural glamour and be known for his guitar expertise. It was a bad time for The Herd, and Peter was both the cause for their discontent as well as the man hardest hit by it. In a way, he had been invited to join the band because his own had broken up, and it might seem as if he had come in and taken over, but Peter was far from a usurper. He was as baffled and frustrated by it as the rest of the members. Still an air of bad feelings surrounded them all. Peter drew himself into a shell, spending time only with his family and his girlfriend Mary Lovett.

But, The Herd's popularity continued to flourish. When they went to concerts, they had to run in and out for fear of being molested by their adoring fans. It was a hectic and troublesome life for teenagers, and it was wearing them thin. While Peter was the number one attraction in the band, the other boys knew they owed their popularity in large part to him, yet they wanted to be recognized as important performers themselves. They certainly deserved to be, and it was definitely not Peter's fault that they weren't. The fault lay within the structure of the business people and the fans. Nevertheless, this was the crux of The Herd's problem.

Peter, himself, was growing "tired, bored and embarrassed by the constant attention." When he went home, he would listen to George Benson, Wes Montgomery, and Kenny Burrell and dream of the future when he would be a jazz guitarist. Yet, he was in a peculiar predicament. He was aware that The Herd's success depended on his presence, but his own happiness was suffering. He was disappointed with himself, disappointed with the direction his music was taking, and unhappy with the group. The life he was leading was not right for him. When he listened to Stevie Wonder and the Beatles, his two rock and blues favorites, he was painfully aware of the way that they had grown as musicians. Stevie Wonder, in particular, was Peter's idol. He had started out as a performing child, in much the same way that Peter had. Yet, Stevie continued to grow and change as he grew in years. Peter was afraid of getting stuck in a rut which would mark him and deny his growth.

As was inevitable, The Herd split up, but it was Peter who precipitated the split. After taking a vacation, during which he spent most of his time musing over the pros and cons of his career, he returned to England and announced his resignation from the group. He continued the last few concerts that were planned and made sure that he didn't leave them up a creek, but he told them he was out. There was no big stir, as the fan magazines had been predicting, just a simple ending. It was for the best, and all concerned agreed. Certain members of the group remained friendly

Madison Square Garden, NYC, 1976   *Chuck Pulin*

toward him, and Andy Bown continued as the closest of Peter's associates. It was all for the best, although the band was forced to close up shop.

At their last meeting, when they gathered to divide their joint profits, they were faced with a rude awakening. They had been cheated out of nearly all of their money. Bad management was responsible, plus the fact that they had taken little interest in their financial affairs. They believed that their managers had been holding money for them in special bank accounts. But they discovered that this was far from the truth. There was no money for them. "Our managers had been fair to us," Peter says, "more fair than our production company, but they never managed us for longevity purposes, they never looked ahead. They never said 'We'll put this away for the group so that when they stop having hits they'll be all right.' "

Peter had been expecting to walk away from The Herd with a tidy sum which would hold him over until he could pick himself up again and choose his next direction. What he and the other boys got, though, was nothing. They were all flat broke and it was a cruel lesson.

"And the killer was," Peter declares, "that my milkman had predicted our demise. He was always delivering the milk when I was arriving home from all-night gigs, and he kept asking me 'Where's your Rolls-Royce?' And then it sort of struck me that there were all these other people riding around in limousines, and I still had a Morris Minor. I couldn't afford to buy anything fantastic for myself, I was earning peanuts — my same fifteen pounds a week. When The Herd broke up we found we had been royally screwed."

This was when Peter learned about the other side of the music business. Of course there are two: the performer himself, and the business people. If you're naive, and young, as were Peter, Andy Bown, Andrew Steele, and Gary Taylor, then you're bound to make mistakes. But you're bound to learn from them too, and that Peter did. Today, he keeps track of his own finances. Although he can't tell you the exact status of his bank account today, he is aware of all his business contracts and deals, which is the lesson he learned when The Herd split up.

The split from The Herd left more scars than just financial. For a long time afterwards, Peter preferred not to discuss it because so many bad feelings were involved. But now, he can look back and say, "I'm tending these days not to regret anything. If it had anything to do with reaching the point I've reached, it was worthwhile. And believe me, I never thought I'd say that."

HUMBLE PIE

After leaving The Herd, Peter had plenty of doubts. Although he felt a release from the anxieties which were destroying him, and he could spend more time with Mary, he was plagued with doubts. Was it right to leave when he did? Did he desert his friends? Was he to blame for the collapse of the group after his departure?

He wasn't sure of just what he would do next. Prior to his leaving the group, Steve Marriott, a key member of the fabulous group Small Faces, had suggested that Peter leave The Herd to form a band of his own. Steve advised Peter of an excellent drummer, a friend of his, Jerry Shirley. Eventually the two got together. Once word was out in the music world that Peter was in the market for a band, musicians by the dozens contacted him.

Although he wasn't quite sure of what he wanted, he knew one thing: this new group would be innovative. They would be equal partners in an effort to grow and experiment musically. Peter was looking to form a band which would feel dynamic, a band which would inspire and excite him as much as The Herd did when he first joined them. But he was determined to learn from the mistakes he had made with his two previous bands.

This new band would not give in to commercialism, and they would not allow the fans to rule them. This new band would create a dynamic energy which would know no bounds. It would feed off its own energy to constantly create a new and vibrant sound, to include jazz, blues, pop and rock.

One momentous afternoon, it was New Year's Day 1969, Steve Marriott called Peter up saying, "Can I join your band? I've quit the Small Faces. And I've also got a great bass player from Spooky Tooth named Greg Ridley." Peter said yes, and then, as he puts it, they were "born!" They called themselves Humble Pie, and the four got together for a month in a country cottage to work out their ideas.

Peter was thrilled with the idea of working with Steve, who he felt was at exactly the same turning point in his career. Both had been in promising bands which ended by bowing to commercial styles. Both had expressed sincere yearnings to delve beyond salable songs and to resist the usual pitfalls with all their might. They were sure that as a team they could really surpass all goals that even they themselves would set.

"I just wanted to be in an exciting rock band for a change and be the guitarist rather than the front man. We wanted to get away from the teeny-boppers and play some serious rock music."

Both Steve and Peter were full of infectious enthusiasm and, as soon as word leaked out about the new group, rock reporters came in droves to get the scoop. Before Humble Pie had uttered a single note of music, they had been billed as the next supergroup. Everyone felt that there was simply no way that the band could miss with the dynamic talents within it.

This media-inspired expectation may now, in retrospect, be viewed as the first pitfall along the bumpy course which Humble Pie followed. But they were not responsible for all the things being printed about them. They said this; "We won't be doing normal gigs. We'd like to do concerts. We don't want to go through all the old scenes." They were very enthusiastic and anxious to merge their ideas and explore their joint musical capabilities. Ideas were exploding in their heads, and it was all they could do to keep from bounding over with the intense excitement that surrounded them. But they wanted to make sure that audiences, as well as the press, knew just what they were all about. There would be no mistaking it; Humble Pie would be the group which would know no limits.

When their first songs hit the market, no one was disappointed. Most importantly, Peter was pleased — at first, that is.

The four boys decided to retreat to an old castle-like cottage where they could practice all night or all day, as they pleased, and trade ideas freely. Staying together to work in a house was Peter's idea, and it is one which he still employs and enjoys a great deal. He feels that it allows the band to exchange thoughts, to work on songs, and to create in a free and comfortable atmosphere. It certainly worked that way for Humble Pie. The more time they spent at their cottage in Essex, the less time they wanted to spend outside of it.

They were generating a great deal of material, and their band was really getting together. It was sounding like a unit of musicians, just as they had planned.

Because they had received such a lot of excited publicity, and because an expectant crowd awaited their first record, they took great pains to keep their initial recording sessions secret. They were not anxious to have members of the press at their early practices. It was important for them to explore just how far their talents and creativity could take them before anyone had the chance to hear them. Then, when they felt confident that

they had taken shape, they would open up to the critics. But first, they needed time to fool around.

They constantly made sure that the public knew not to expect the "same old stuff" from Humble Pie and tried to remind themselves that, above all else, they themselves would not become trapped by the media hype which had already begun.

Most of Humble Pie's material was generated by Peter and Steve. They were the two bandleaders, and they were the two driving forces behind the group. To be sure, Greg and Jerry were important members, but there would be a clear delineation of responsibility. In that way, they hoped to overcome the problems that plagued The Herd, where there were too many equal partners and no director-type. Steve and Peter would handle all decision making together, and they agreed on that — at first.

By the end of the Pie's first summer together, they had created enough material to put out their first album, *As Safe As Yesterday*. They had already been nicknamed "The Piemen" by the press, and the whole music world anxiously awaited the LP's release. It was a smash success, and the song released as a single "Natural Born Boogie," raced its way to the top of the charts. What a thrill it was for Peter to see the group's first efforts so well received. Yet, he was very careful to guard against the same atmosphere which surrounded The Herd. He did not want the new group to be locked into the style of its first album and single. He did not want the public to expect that Humble Pie would necessarily continue to create music which was true to any previous Humble Pie style. At this point, their sound was hard, heavy rock, personified by Peter's expert guitar playing. They were easily England's hottest band. It was decided that a small European tour would help further expose the group, so the boys planned a tour of Belgium, Holland, Germany and England. Peter's bad memories of concerts immediately came to mind when he thought of the tour.

As a member of The Herd, giving concerts had become a thing to dread. Running into the hall, under cover of their instruments to avoid being attacked by fans, The Herd would find themselves onstage being screamed at so loudly by the audience that no one could hear their singing or playing. It was a very depressing, as well as frightening, experience. So, when Peter thought of touring with the Piemen, he was apprehensive.

Nevertheless, it was for the good of the band. The four had become very close; there was a true friendship among them. They were dedicated to making Humble Pie work for all of them. They were all as interested in having a creative and experimental band as he was. It would be worth it to tour, if it would help the band gain the freedom to continue to explore.

Although he was not anxious to repeat that same hit single, "Natural Born Boogie", over and over again, he felt that he would go along. And sure enough, that first tour brought them even closer together. The stage suited the creative energy which Peter and Steve brought out in each other. They enjoyed working on stage and, although Peter found himself more and more on the side while Steve assumed a more prominent position, he didn't mind. He was pleased to be in the background a bit and was happy just to work at his guitar and not have to sing. Singing was Steve's job; so, if he took a front position, that was all right by Peter.

However, Peter noticed that Steve's dominance was beginning to surface in other areas as well. It seemed that with every passing decision which the group had to make, it was Steve who had the most important say, and Peter, though he was an equal partner, had a much less important voice. Because he enjoyed the friendships of the band, and because he loved jamming with them, he refused to acknowledge that a split was taking place. We might, of course, have guessed that two willful personalities would find it hard to keep a perfect balance of power. Steve cannot necessarily be blamed for the way he gradually took over, for it was as much a part of his personality as it was a part of Peter's to choose to ignore

Frampton's Camel 1974   *Chuck Pulin*

it. This problem coupled with the fact that Humble Pie began to fall directly into the same trap they had expressly wished to avoid.

No sooner had they completed their successful British tour, (the first Holland and Belgium tours were disasters,) than they found they were in demand to give concerts and to get back on the road. "Natural Born Boogie"was such a huge success, that they began to mold their next tunes in that style. Soon, they had become England's number one "heavy metal" band and were as branded by a style as could be. Naturally, Peter was once again frustrated by his situation. He found himself, for the second time, to be in a highly successful band that was content to turn out a single type of music based on a single successful formula. Of course, this time he was reaping the monetary profits, and he and his buddies enjoyed that. During the years he spent with Humble Pie, Peter bought himself a large house in England and a wonderful sportscar, an Aston-Martin.

The more the Pie toured doing the same deafening material, the more dissatisfied Peter grew, and he began thinking of leaving the group. They put out another album entitled *Town & Country*, again a big hit, and then they were offered an American tour. This kept Peter with the band. He had been extremely interested in visiting the United States.

The band felt that going to the U.S. might allow them the chance to play some of their acoustic numbers, but unfortunately, the American audiences wanted only hard rock. They were welcomed by the audiences, but Peter was getting tired of playing only that type of material. Their American debut was at the legendary Fillmore East, a concert hall which was a special and important stop for any group. They played as the second act for Santana, and, even in the shadow of such a supergroup, Humble Pie received an extremely warm welcome. At the end of their set, Steve and Peter were given a standing ovation, insuring them of their continued American success.

As the band toured America, Peter became enthralled by all of the music Americans have available to them. He loved listening to the radio — there were so many stations and so many types of music to hear. His favorite American music was Motown, but, as for rock, he felt that England still had the upper hand. Before he left England, Peter had been given so many warnings about America that he was quite afraid of finding murderers, muggers, bums, and filth all over the streets. He soon learned that this was not all as he had been led to believe, but he still wasn't sure of just how safe America was. He called Mary every day to tell her how things were and to share his stories of America with her. They had decided to get married when he returned. Although their relationship had been having its ups and

JFK Stadium, Philadelphia, 1977   *Chuck Pulin*

downs, they had been together for nearly five years, and neither could imagine life without the other. They were married in 1970, when Peter returned to England from that first American tour.

He and Mary set up a home and being a newlywed consoled Peter, although he wondered if Humble Pie was the right group for him. The group's third album, *Humble Pie*, was even more successful than the previous two, and it was this album which helped to establish Peter with a following of his own. One of the biggest hits from this album was a tune entitled "Walk on Gilded Splinters," in which Peter's slick guitar work was allowed to shine alone.

The number of Humble Pie's fans continued to increase, and Peter couldn't simply get up and leave in the midst of such tremendous success. He was an important aspect of the entire group even if he was not the leader he had intended to be. The group was no longer his and Steve's alone, but it was, nevertheless, a real crowd pleaser. Their next album, *Rock On* continued with the "heavy metal" sound and was a success. Peter's two songs from this LP, "The Light" and "Shine On" were the favorite tunes from the album, and even today he includes "Shine On" in his act. However, he had written some acoustic numbers which he was unable to fit into the Humble Pie sound. This kind of music was the direction he wished to pursue, and he was growing continually frustrated by the fact that he could not find an outlet for the diversity of his creative talents.

Eventually, he had to confront the group with the problem. Humble Pie had been formed dedicated to continued creative exploration; instead, they had found a profitable and tremendously accepted niche and stuck there. None of the other members wanted to stray from the path which had been so good to them. They decided that until the public was tired of their sound, they would stay that way.

This was not what Peter wanted to hear. But Jerry and Greg were in agreement with Steve, and it seemed that Peter's vote didn't count. He was no longer a part-leader; Steve was the accepted leader. Peter knew that he could not stay with the band, no matter how successful they had become. He needed to explore other musical avenues, and he was not satisfied with being merely an underling in a band which he himself had created.

"I left Humble Pie because I was interested in leading my own band, and there wasn't really room for two leaders in one band. Steve and I just couldn't compete," Peter said.

"Musically, I just wasn't into heavy rock and roll anymore. Steve was going into more R & B stuff, and our music was just moving apart instead of moving even more tightly together. I wanted to do acoustic things that I'd written, and that wouldn't have worked out being a member of Humble Pie. So I had to leave."

In retrospect, it was a simple decision. But, at the time it was agonizing. The disappointment of having given birth to a band for which Peter had grand intentions and then to lose it to the other members, was a grievous situation. When he realized that he wasn't in control, and he wasn't satisfied with the direction Humble Pie was taking, he felt he had no choice but to leave.

For his next band, whenever that would happen, he would be in charge, and only he. Peter contacted Dee Anthony, the Pie's manager, and told him of his decision to quit. While Peter had been arguing with the band, while he had been racked with indecision about his role and the band's direction, he had turned more and more to Dee for friendship. So, it was only fair that Peter inform Dee of his decision. Dee, rather than becoming upset with Peter, offered to manage him as a solo act. This was a real show of support and encouragement at a time when Peter needed it most. He was depressed about the Humble Pie situation, and he was having problems with Mary that the marriage hadn't settled.

It was a time when Peter needed every sincere friend he could muster. And Dee provided him with just that sort of friendship. In fact, Peter's friendship with Dee has remained one of the brightest points in his life. It was Dee who encouraged Peter through all the hard years as he struggled to become recognized as a soloist; Dee who lent Peter the money to finance most of his solo albums; and Dee who suggested that Peter throw all of his energy into touring in order to strengthen his already strong rapport with his audiences. This last suggestion is perhaps the most evident reason for Peter's recent phenomenal success. But their friendship has surpassed a purely business level. Both men share a lasting friendship which includes seeking each other out for advice on personal matters and sharing personal happiness. When Dee's daughter, Michelle, graduated recently from George Washington University, in Washington, D.C., Peter flew to be there. Both men sport matching diamond earrings which they gave to each other as gifts.

But the fact remained that Dee was there when Peter needed a friend and a confidante, and for a performer that is rare. Today, Dee claims that he knew all along that Peter would make it big on his own terms. But did he suspect just how big?

After Peter left the Pie, they continued to tour without their lead guitartist, and, naturally the press picked up on this conspicuous absence. When Peter was pressed to explain his sudden split, he chose to reply simply and not to air his gripes. He said, "I didn't contribute more than one or two songs per album because what I was writing really wasn't suited to Humble Pie's identity." He stressed the fact that his ambitions had begun to steer him in a different musical direction, and he played down any personal differences between himself and Steve or Jerry and Greg.

Just as Peter left the group, they released their live album, *Rockin' The Fillmore*. All of the band members had known that this album would really make it big. It has always been a part of Dee's philosophy that, after a group is successful, a live album will help to give a larger audience the feel of being at a concert, as well as to remind concert-goers of how exciting it was to be there.

As predicted, *Rockin' The Fillmore* rose to the top of the charts, and although Peter had left the group knowing that it would, it gave him cause to question the logic of his decision. "I clutched my heart as I watched this thing shoot to the top of the charts. It was a gold album within three weeks. I thought, 'Uh-oh, Pete's made a boo-boo.' But in the end, it made me want to leave Humble Pie even more."

Actually, although Peter knew that the album would be big, he simply didn't know the extent of the popularity it would have. One of the prime reasons for leaving when he did, was that he preferred not to be tied so intricately to that album. It was the epitome of the Humble Pie sound which

he had grown so frustrated with. Although he would, of course, be noted for his excellent contributions on this album — among them the song "Walk on Gilded Splinters" — he had hoped that, by extricating himself from the group at that time, he would leave himself free to be judged on his own merits.

As the album continued to gain prominence, many fans asked if Peter might rejoin the group. But he stuck to his initial reasons for leaving and reminded the public that Humble Pie simply did not allow him to work in all the musical genres he wished to. He did not bring any of the personality conflicts between himself and Steve Marriott into public discussions, but while Peter was guarding himself from airing their differences, Marriott was giving vent to the hard feelings among them.

The other members of the band felt that Peter's departure would be a signal to the fans and the press that Humble Pie had begun to crumble. "All wasn't well with Humble Pie," Peter says now, "but my leaving had to be." Steve freely attributed many problems to Peter, even though that was far from the truth. He claimed that Peter was a hard man to get along with and that he insisted on being the front man in the group. Of course, this was the complete opposite of reality, because when Humble Pie was formed, Peter wanted nothing more than to be the side man on stage.

But, as he watched the rise of the Pie, he realized that, in the future, any new band would have to be under his direction. It was impossible to maintain dual leadership.

Sometime later, Marriott decided to find a replacement for Peter because the Pie as a trio wasn't working out. They needed that second strong lead guitar, and they began to search for a man who could play driving lead, but remain in the background as far as group politics was concerned. They found Dave "Clem" Clemson, formerly with the British group Colosseum, and he eased right into the spot. He picked up his parts easily and seemed the perfect replacement for Peter. Humble Pie's fans loved "Clem" and it seemed the group was back together again. Marriott made no pretense about his happiness with Clemson and let the world know that Humble Pie was prepared to rock on, conceivably forever.

Unfortunately, Humble Pie just wasn't the same without Peter, and their next album *Smokin'* wasn't up to par. *Rolling Stone* recommended that it be used as a frisbee. Peter was definitely an integral part of the band; his virtuoso guitar work helped to make their music dynamic. The group's collapse, however, may be attributed to more than that alone. Perhaps audiences were tiring, as was Peter, of that hard-driving style of rock.

STUDIO WORK —
BEGINNING OF SOLO CAREER

Twice Peter had been a key member of an extremely successful band, and twice — at the peak of success — he had opted out. Both times he left purely for reasons of integrity; the bands were not remaining true to themselves. They were satisfied to accept the adulation of the audience rather than risk losing it by attempting to expand their musical repertoires. For Peter, this was musical suicide. Whether or not an audience would accept the new styles he would try remained to be proven; however, he had to experiment for his own well-being.

Some critics wondered aloud whether Peter sincerely expected his audiences to follow him as he drifted from group to group. But, it was time for his fans to see the entire panorama of Frampton's musical ability; time to hear his acoustic numbers, his ballads, and folky tunes, as well as the hard rock they already knew he could execute so well.

Peter now needed time to think out his plans. He needed time to reflect on how to approach starting his new career. Luckily, his share of the profits from Humble Pie's records was enough to keep him and Mary going for quite a while, and he could have that necessary time to ponder his future. There were two facets of his life which needed clearing up at that time. First of all, his marriage was on shaky ground, and now that he was freed from the incessant touring with the band, he hoped that he and Mary could manage to regain what had been the dearest thing in both their lives. It was this touring which had been the crux of their problems. While Mary was as patient and understanding as is possible, it was getting more and more difficult for her to remain on the sidelines during all the months of touring. With Peter home for a while, they hoped that their life would settle down. He enjoyed being home again and was glad to be in London, but soon he began to miss working and decided that the best thing for him to do would be to get back in the studio as a session man.

Fortunately, his good name had lost none of the sparkle, and he was none the worse for having left the Pie. Peter was asked to play back-up for many prominent musicians. He found himself working for Harry Nilsson on his *Son of Schmilsson* album and for George Harrison on his *All Things*

Must Pass album. He also worked for Tim Hardin, John Entwistle and Nicky Hopkins.

Session work was very rewarding for Peter at first. He was able to play a number of styles depending on which artists he worked with. It was both relaxing and envigorating. Many fine musicians are satisfied to work in this capacity for their entire careers and a large number of today's better-known artists began this way. But after a while Peter grew anxious to do his own material.

While he was doing session work, he was writing songs for himself and thinking about which musicians he wanted to work with on his first solo album. While session work was "very, very interesting," Peter ached for a creative outlet that would be totally his own. This would be a true adventure, for while Peter had proven his talents countless numbers of times within the framework of a group, there was really no indication that he could make it as a soloist.

There was never any question of Peter's competence, but a solo performer needs more than ability to succeed. A soloist must have stage presence, must be able to capture an audience's attention, and be able to hold it. As a soloist, Peter would have to project his personality to the audience in order that they could find a common ground on which to relate to him. He would have to do more than just go on stage and play excellent guitar, he would have to present a cohesive program held together by music as well as the man.

While in Humble Pie, Peter had been quite happy with remaining in the background on stage. His guitar came alive, and although the fans knew it was Peter plucking at the strings, they didn't need wild showmanship on his part to prove it. But with Peter in charge of his own act, he would have to step out more and make himself seen center stage.

"It took a long time after Humble Pie to just get up on stage and do all my own stuff and be the front man," Peter said. "To start with, it scared me to death, but the more we worked, the more confidence I got."

Dee Anthony was behind Peter all the way. From the moment Peter let him know he was ready to strike out on his own, Dee began to do his part. Dee knew it would take a considerable amount of time and energy for Peter to gain the status he sought as a soloist, and he knew that Peter would have to tour in order to promote himself. He was ready to help Peter build the confidence and courage necessary to control a show.

"When I first left Humble Pie," Peter said, "I thought 'I'm not going to go on the road again. I'm just going to record and sit back.' But after six months, I was anxious and wanted to get back on the road quickly."

To begin with, Peter needed a fresh image. In England he was still living under the shadow of "Face of 68," and he felt it was important to "go somewhere I wasn't known as a teen idol." Dee was based in America, and to work closely with Dee, would mean to live in the U.S. For both of these reasons, Peter and Mary moved to America. They took a home forty miles outside of New York City in a lovely wooded area that reminded them of favorite spots in England. They also hoped that this new home would mean a fresh start for their marriage. Mary was Peter's strongest advocate at this time and that devotion helped him to attack his new solo career with vigor.

For the next several months, Peter prepared the material for his first solo

Chuck Pulin

album, which he called *Wind of Change*. The title alone suggests both the departure Peter took from working with rigid groups, as well as the variety of music which he would present on the LP. Of all his solo efforts, Peter's favorite is this album, his first. "I think *Wind of Change* was really important because I had a long time to spend preparing the material, about five or six months after Humble Pie, to do nothing but think of my own ventures. I wanted more experience doing sessions with other people, and in the process, met Ringo while I was doing *All Things Must Pass* with George Harrison. I remember asking Ringo if he would play on an album of mine and playing some of my songs on acoustic guitar for him. Let me tell you, playing your songs for one of the Beatles is an experience! Nervous? Just a trifle! Once I knew I had Ringo, that was a start. Then A & M had just gotten Billy Preston, and I was introduced to him. Klaus Voorman was there, and they both agreed to play on the album."

So, with the assurance that his album would have top-notch musicians, Peter felt that, if nothing else, it would be a tight and professional work. Peter produced this album entirely himself, and he is an exacting perfectionist in the studio. At times, he can drive his musicians right up the wall, making them repeat songs again and again, but knowing that he is in control of his own project keeps him constantly on his toes. He wants to be sure that only the best of their efforts are put onto the record.

The lyrics Peter writes invariably deal with the feelings and events which Peter is experiencing at the time. *Wind of Change* speaks of his marriage with Mary and his new beginning as a solo performer. Critics have often said his lyrics tend to be banal, shallow, and simple; but even so, they are engaging, and the critics admit so. Simple as they may be, they combine with Peter's inimitable melodic style of music to make songs which many people of all ages and types do enjoy and relate to. That is the key: to make songs which your audience can feel. It is a talent which Peter has been nurturing and which grew with each successive song he penned. "As Pete Townshend said," Peter says, "the secret to reaching people is to use your own experiences, which are everybody's experiences, and try to put a little message across. I'm not going to tell people what to do; I'm just giving them what's happened to me so that they can relate to my music."

This philosophy seems to have worked extremely well for Peter because, more than simply having fans, Peter's fans feel they know him — that he is singing to them and about them.

Peter feels that his lyrics are the worst thing he does. While the critics may agree with him, his words are a great vehicle for involving the audience totally in his music. On *Wind of Change*, the first song recorded was "The Lodger" a rocking number which featured Ringo on drums. "All Right," using Ringo's percussion and Billy Preston's dynamic keyboard artistry, was another rocker. "Fig Tree Bay" makes use of innovative rhythms. The greatest aspect of this album is its tremendous variety. It includes quiet, melodic numbers as well as those more standard rock and roll tunes. While this album was an experimental venture into these varieties of music which Peter enjoys, it also made it harder for audiences to accept it. Peter's version of "Jumping Jack Flash" was such a departure. It was included at the suggestion of Andy Bown, who had by this time become a well-versed studio man and arranger, and was present for Peter's solo session. "Jack

Frampton's Camel   *Chuck Pulin*

Flash'' sounds so far from the original Stones hard-driving rock version, that some felt it was murdering the song. Peter's handling of the tune did give it a more melodic, almost pleasant sound, and today he ends his shows with this song. It has become a true crowd pleaser in the Frampton style. One critic exclaimed in surprise that Peter is able to make "Jumping Jack Flash" sound like a friendly song.

The critics, nevertheless, welcomed this first effort from the boy who had been a teen-hero. Many suggested that it would be voted the best album of 1972, and that it would make Peter Frampton one of the biggest performers in rock. Peter himself was quite pleased with the results of his move to the more acoustic, sweet sound he had always wanted to do. When he read what the papers had to say about his LP, he couldn't have been more excited. *Rolling Stone* claimed that Peter had proven to be "among the most enjoyable solo artists to emerge lately," and the album did indeed make nearly every best records of the year list.

But despite all the good publicity, *Wind of Change* did not sell well. Perhaps one reason for this problem was that none of the cuts made it as a single. While all were good tunes and did get their share of airplay, none was played consistently and featured as a single. Like it or not, it is often single cuts, those which receive continuous airplay for an extended period of time, that make album sales soar. Usually, an infectious and perhaps representative tune is released as a single; the radio stations give it repeated play, and if it is admired by the public, it is requested over and over. Then, they get curious and they buy the album to hear that cut at home as well as to find out what else their new-found artist has done.

Wind of Change, however, showcased no one particular style of Peter's musicianship, but gave vent to the variety of creations which had been brewing within him for so long. The public had been used to albums which organize themselves around a certain theme or style. The fact that this time-honored formula had been ignored may have led to the album's being passed over by the public. Today, however, with Peter's amazing success, his fans are rediscovering his first album and wondering why they never paid attention to it before.

Although the reviews had been great, the album just didn't sell. A & M records and Dee Anthony set out to do something about this.

While it would have been nice had the album really taken off, Peter was well aware of the time and effort it would take for his career to bloom. "If *Wind of Change* had been a hit album, for me it would have been a mental home job — just too much of a strain. I wouldn't have been ready for it."

The next step in building up Peter's recognition with the fans, now that the critics knew who he was, was to get his show on the road. He did not have a formal band, and getting one would be his first priority. Peter says, "Dee sort of dropped the hint, as a parent, 'I think you ought to think about playing in front of the public in the U.S. because your album is in the record stores.'"

At this point Peter formed his band which he called Frampton's Camel. The name was an unpretentious title for the group, and it was chosen partly because Peter wished expressly not to be tied to any pretty-boy connotations.

The band, which Peter took to the road, was a tight group of musicians, good friends and aware of the fact that Peter was the final decision maker. Mick Gallagher was on keyboards, Rick Wills on bass, and John Siomos on drums. Together they charmed concert audiences as they toured city after city and town after town, as the warm-up act for some of the better known bands. At one point, they even shared a bill with Humble Pie, and the Camel was well received. Reviews were glowing; the critics praised everything from Peter's masterful guitar playing to the talents of each of the band members to the show which was clean, and non-theatrical. Touring was tiring, but the good reviews helped to boost Peter's confidence.

He remembered that touring was one of the best ways to bring your music to the people. The singing was wearing him thin, however, and he began to suffer from doing the constant vocals. He had been used to sharing the vocals or remaining as a secondary vocalist. Now with his own band, he was the premier vocalist and his throat was in pain. He had never had any singing instruction, and he soon wished that he could get some lessons, but the heavy scheduling of the Camel's touring did not permit that. The main singing lesson Peter learned he attributes to singer Peter Wolf of the J. Geils Band. That lesson was that singing should come from the diaphragm rather than the throat. From this elementary singing lesson,

1974   *Chuck Pulin*

Peter was able to utilize his voice more fully and to sing without tearing his throat up. With each successive performance, his vocals sounded stronger and more assured.

With all of the touring the Camel did, Peter knew what would suffer most: his marriage. It was unfortunate, but true, that he and Mary had never really solved their differences, and that his renewed touring could only make matters worse. But that was the way it had to be. In order for his career to take off, he had to tour and, although Mary understood that, the long months away made them seem like strangers to each other when he returned. When he completed this first tour with the Camel, he came home to find that there was just no way to make the marriage work. The intense love that characterized their early years had faded. Although neither wanted to let the other go, they knew that the best thing would be to separate while they still had respect for each other.

This was a shattering experience for both of them, but at least for Peter, he could work out his pain in his music. His second album, *Frampton's Camel,* dealt with this devastating break-up. Each one of the songs speaks of the painful process of losing a relationship, of losing love, and, for anyone who has ever had such an experience, the lyrics are only too touching. There is no blame, no vindictiveness, because if anything, Peter blamed himself for losing their love. The songs simply relate the eerie feelings, the painful moments, and shattering emotions he experienced.

"Lines On My Face," by now one of Peter's classic tunes, is an anguished cry to the woman he lost, and "Which Way the Wind Blows" is a plaintive telling of a man who is a stranger in the old familiar places he and his wife once shared. "Don't Fade Away" and "All Night Long" are sorrowful tunes in which he cries to her to keep him within her heart and to share love together once again. While this album is the most intensely personal of all of his albums, its revealing lyrics have an enchanting and bitter-sweet professionalism. They are among the most frightening and endearing lyrics he has written. This album established him as a lyricist, as well as bringing to the fore, once again, his sensational musicianship. The lyrics are beautiful and the music which accompanies them is equally eerie and thrilling.

Frampton's Camel was a success with the critics, and the one song released as a single — the one which is happy, and totally unlike the rest of the tunes — "Do You Feel Like We Do?" (in which the band asks the audience if it feels as happy and as excited as they do) made it to the singles charts. Today, this song is the ultimate crowd pleaser in Peter's repertoire during which fans stand to cheer and sing along.

The critics loved the album, praising Peter for his outstanding guitar work and his ever-improving lyrics, but the album just didn't sell well. Peter had to do something to promote higher sales, or it would be difficult for him to continue to produce albums. His funds were at a low point, and it was expensive to keep a band on the road. Finally, the decision was made for Peter to move permanently to America. He had been jogging back and forth between England and America, and because of that and the British taxes his financial resources were drained.

America was the logical place to go, as the music of the 1970's was emanating from there. At least Peter didn't have to make the move alone. Mary moved too. Now that they had decided that their marriage just couldn't work, they had been having an easier time of simply being friends. The best part of their relationship had been the devotion and friendship that they had given each other, and luckily for them, the ending of their marriage didn't stop that.

With Dee Anthony and with Mary, Peter would have just about all the friends he would need in America. He had always loved the country because he felt it has such a wealth of music. Peter had always been impressed with the multitude of radio stations offering a diversity of music, and that certainly appealed to him. The British political scene was

Frampton's Camel 1973   *Chuck Pulin*

depressing to him as well, and that was another facet in finalizing his move away from his homeland. In fact, there were so many factors involved in this move, that when Peter was asked by the British press if he was deserting England, he replied, "No." Although he admitted that the British tax system was eating up most of his profits, he also said, "America gives me a lot of inspiration."

"It's mainly a personal thing," he stressed. "The old music business can wreck personal lives." He then explained that he felt it was time to devote himself entirely to his music if need be, at the expense of his personal life. It was time for Peter to make another fresh start.

With Peter settling in America, he would have to work long and hard to solve the problem of having critical acclaim and live performance acceptance, yet poor record sales.

Upon moving, he endeavored once again, to keep his name and his music in front of the public. He resumed his incessant touring and spent nearly all of his time on the road. Gradually, he found a warmer and more familiar reception when he returned to cities where he had previously played. He was most gracious about giving interviews and became a favorite with all the local disc-jockeys. He was making his personality known and was being rewarded in a small way for his niceness. Yet, it took much more than niceness. Peter had to spend much of his time on the road to gain the widespread popularity he now enjoys.

Peter toured non-stop and began thinking about his next album, but he couldn't write on the road, so, in order to produce the next LP, he needed some time off.

He had found a new girlfriend, Penny McCall (the former wife of one of Peter's roadies) and happiness had drifted back into his life. She inspired Peter to write new songs which reflected his new love and growing confidence. Peter's third solo album, *Somethin's Happening* appeared in 1974. Some critics were disappointed with this album, claiming that the production was not as professional as his two previous works and that his lyrics lacked "conviction." But, *Billboard* magazine immediately placed the album on its "recommended" list, praising Peter's expert guitar work and vocals. The tune released as a single was the title tune. Although it didn't make it big at the time, it is today another of Peter's anthems. It is an infectious song with mounting rhythm, which catches the audiences' spirits and creates a joyous mood.

Critics said that on this album Peter's guitar work was "impeccable." If nothing else, he was raising himself up another notch in the esteem of his peers and the press. Unfortunately, again, the album was not a big seller.

Peter's solo career remained as a mystery. Why was this supremely talented and well-loved young man able to please live audiences, produce excellent albums, and yet not sell them? Even Peter's musical peers professed to be confounded by this. Nearly everyone in the rock world acknowledged Peter's expertise. His work was getting slicker; but for some reason the fans weren't buying his albums. There was simply no answer to be found as to why his solo career had not taken off.

Peter's growing confidence from touring was justifiably gained. They loved him in person, yet, when he saw that his albums weren't making sales, he began to worry that his career wasn't going anywhere.

Frampton's Camel   1973   *Chuck Pulin*

Financial pressures began setting in. It was extremely expensive to keep the band on tour, yet necessary if he were ever to gain the acclaim he needed. Borrowing money was something he did not relish doing, but he had no other choice. Fortunately, Dee did not mind lending Peter the money he needed, and until his *Alive!* album, Peter was in debt to Dee for nearly a quarter-of-a-million dollars. "It got to the point where I couldn't borrow any more money to lose," says Peter.

Originally, *Somethin's Happening* was the album meant to break Peter through the gloom which had spread over his career. "Looking back, I can see the weaknesses," Peter says, "but watching that album fizzle out and disappear was so painful. That was the most disheartening of anything. That was the point where it was almost back to being a session man. I definitely thought about it. Heavily."

Peter claims that his next album was done out of desperation. Strangely enough, it was this, his fourth solo album, *Frampton*, which helped to get him out of his rut. This album was widely received and, best of all, it started the momentum for the big breakthrough. The public bought this album, and Peter was able to see his way out of the debt and desperation which had been hanging over him.

Electric Light Orchestra, NYC, 1977   *Chuck Pulin*

Frampton was recorded in an old castle near Gloucester. Clearwater Castle was a wonderful place to record, and the band enjoyed it thoroughly. Peter felt that living and working in the same place gave them the freedom to allow their creativity to flow. "We could start whenever we wanted and eat whenever we wanted. We never felt like 'God, we gotta get back to the grindstone, we're wasting money.'" (Studio time is incredibly expensive.) "When we really got into something, we'd work twelve hours straight and come out with three tracks; so, it was worth it. When you're tired, you just climb upstairs and go to bed. When you wake up you can go for a walk in the garden." Peter attributes the flow of this album to that relaxed atmosphere, and he claims that the lovely sounds are directly related to the castle itself.

The opening cut on the album, "Day's Dawning," uses the chirping birds outside of the castle which awakened the boys. "We had a mike outside because the day was dawning, and I wrote the words around a crowing rooster." Peter found every aspect of the castle inspiring. "I'm very much against the dead studio sound," Peter says, "which made the ambience of the rooms in the castle perfect for the recordings. Even in a studio, we put the drums in (a room) alone and use the whole room sound, so we don't

54

need to add any echo electronically. In the castle, we all went around clapping our hands to find which rooms were right for which instruments. It was a terrific experience."

Peter produced this album himself, and he has a right to be proud of this accomplishment. In his own assessment of the album, he says, "It sounds competent, it sounds happy, it sounds as if I know what I'm doing, whereas *Somethin's Happening* was a bit more out there; it wasn't quite as together." As for the critics' reactions, he says, "Some people like it, some people don't, but I feel it's professional. I'm learning all the time, and I'm sure there's a million lessons to be learned in the next three . . . weeks!"

The critics stood behind Peter's own impressions, claiming that the exuberant songs were dynamic, well executed, and as exciting as anything else they'd heard. Naturally, the majority of the tunes on this LP revolved around Peter's growing love for Penny, and *Newsweek* said, "She and all those endless nights on the road were apparently the charms that turned his fourth album to near gold in sales and paved the way for *Alive!*"

On the *Frampton* album, Andy Bown played bass, John Siomos was the drummer, and Peter was, of course, guitarist and lead singer. Peter did all the overdubs; in fact, critics have often said that Peter's use of multi-overdubs makes him virtually a one-man-band. Some have said that perhaps it was Peter's inability to gather musicians as talented as he which held him back from an earlier success. They noted that on his albums he often chose to overdub bass, organ, piano and drums himself rather than to trust other musicians.

But once the *Frampton* album was completed, the band took the shape it is now: Stanley Sheldon on bass, Bob Mayo on keyboards, and John Siomos on drums. Now they are a tight unit and very professional. There is a camaraderie among them, and they enjoy working with the material. It shows in their concerts; fans know it.

There is a funny story Peter tells about how he managed to get Bob Mayo into the band. It was December 31, 1975, and Peter was checking into a Holiday Inn in the area where he had been looking for a house to buy. He stepped into the bar to listen to the band and stayed because he thought it sounded pretty good. There was Bob Mayo playing keyboards, and Peter couldn't believe it. They were playing disco. He explains that it was the "peak of the disco time." Peter had known Bob as a friend of a friend; they had met a few times before and had known each other altogether about two or three years. So, Peter said hello to him and even joined the band onstage for a few numbers, including "Jungle Boogie!"

The band was at that Holiday Inn for a week, and since Bob lived near

Peter, they got together to listen to records and talk. "Bob plays keyboards, guitar, and sings," Peter exclaims; so, they decided to try working together in Peter's band for a month. As we all know, it worked.

Although the *Frampton* album helped Peter to regain his spirits, he still was not in a position to sit back and relax. He had to continue on the road, facing his fans, and expanding his audience. Because he was not yet out of debt, and despite the good reactions to *Frampton*, he still had to prove himself to his record company. They had been spending a tremendous amount of money on Peter for quite a few years; they couldn't afford to continue to back him indefinitely unless he made a good showing in sales.

Once again, Peter and the band set off to tour, tour, tour. They did their most recent tunes at each concert. Peter found that the fans knew more of his material than he suspected. The song released as a single, "No Where's Too Far For My Baby To Go," was an often requested song, but Peter's favorite, "Show Me The Way," dedicated to Penny and about learning to love again, had yet to gain its due popularity.

All this touring was getting rather exhausting, but Peter tried not to let it get him down. He preferred just relaxing at home, watching TV, listening to records, walking, and, yes, playing his guitar. Believe it or not, the guitar is still the best way for Peter to relax. But, there would be enough time for all of that once he had assured his future. And after three years of struggling and watching his albums sink, it was worth it one more time to play up the success of the *Frampton* album.

In fact, he had only two choices: either he made an all-out effort on the road again, or he returned to session work. His financial position dictated these choices, and there were really no other choices.

These were desperate times for Peter. While he admits, "I've never been as poor as a million people, I'm not crying poverty," he does say, "But it was bad. Hard to find the rent, things like that."

Earlier in 1975, when Mick Taylor had left the Stones, Peter had been honored by being a top contender for Taylor's replacement. That would have assured him a nice income and guaranteed that his name be known, but Peter didn't want to become involved in another group effort. He wanted to be the front man this time out, and group politics were definitely out of the question; so, he took himself out of the running. Nevertheless, it was a great compliment.

He knew he could do well as a session man, as his talent was highly respected among his peers. Yet, he had the yearning to make it alone in front of an audience. In truth, Peter had an amazing rapport with his audiences, and he could feel that they responded directly to him while he was on stage. Many performers simply play; many put on a show; many use dramatic theatrics but don't communicate with their audiences. They look beyond them. But Peter has mastered the technique of reaching each member of an audience; it is an extension of his warm personality, and it makes concerts rewarding to Peter as much as to his fans. When Peter sings his tunes, he usually finds the audience singing right along with him. There is nothing he appreciates more when giving a show than to see people mouthing the words of his songs. It lets him know that not only did they enjoy his music and take the time to listen to it enough to know the words, but that they also must feel the words as he did when he wrote them.

During the concerts the band did after the release of the *Frampton* album, Peter always thanked the audience for making the album a success by buying it. He says that he thinks that, for many of his fans, it may have felt as if they shared his success with him. He thinks that many felt a part of the whole growing process. Certainly, there are a few performers who appreciate the fans as genuinely as Peter does. This is not to say that Peter is crazy about groupies and others who corner him in the street or throng around his doorway. Naturally, this is an annoyance, and Peter feels trapped by such rudeness. He doesn't mind signing a few autographs or having a chat with someone who passes, but being a star is tough enough without people making it impossible for him to step outside of his home in comfort.

This series of tours may have been tiring, but there can be no doubt that they finalized the ground-breaking he had worked for. By now, he was known; the process was finally paying off. After spending the better part of four years on the road, he had built a loyal following. This following would help to put him over the top. With fingers crossed, Peter began planning his next album. This next album would make him.

FRAMPTON COMES ALIVE!

"Good entertainers perform for their audiences, while great performers entertain their audiences." So said Edgar Gardner in the Sacramento, California, *Rock 'N Roll News*, in describing Peter Frampton's stage presence. An interesting use of words, perhaps, but yet it still doesn't quite capture the vitality Peter puts into his concerts. He does more than simply entertain. He becomes part of the audience's life for those few hours, making the show their show, giving energy, creating excitement, and drawing from the mutual highs of the event. There doesn't seem to be a group of words suitable to explain the intensity of Peter's concerts.

When he uses the voice-bag, or talk-box, now his trademark, fans go crazy. A voice-bag is a method of using the vocal chords with an instrument to produce a voice-like sound from the electric guitar. It's an interesting contraption that allows Peter to speak to his audience personally, and when he brings it out, they hush up to listen. "It's really nice to talk to audiences like that," Peter says. "They don't want to be shouted at like so many groups do. If you communicate subtly, they'll understand you."

Peter explains that the talk-box concept first appeared somewhere around 1925. The talk-box he uses took a number of years to develop. "It's been a secret for a long time, but it's so simple," he says. "The one I use is called a Heil, which is from Bob Heil's sound system. He made one, and instead of a bag over the shoulder, (as had been the way previously) he has a box on the floor. It's quite difficult to use — I couldn't talk with it for a long time. But all it consists of is a small speaker in a box, with a tube coming out of the top leading to your mouth. The box becomes another lung or diaphragm. You just have to over-mouth the words."

If his talk-box is one secret way of communicating with the audience, it is by no means the only one. First and foremost, Peter has a true love for and appreciation of his audiences. "They, the audience, are the most important people." This attitude has been the key to Peter's phenomenal success with live performances.

Now, if he could only capture that excitement on an album, that would surely sell!

Madison Square Garden, NYC, 1976   *Chuck Pulin*

Peter's fifth album was originally planned as a single studio LP with fresh material. He had been pleased with his *Frampton* album, but wanted to surpass it. Peter decided to think on a grander scale. He decided to do a live album that included his best numbers — a representative sampler of Frampton favorites, from hard rock to acoustic. At first, this was a bone of contention between Peter and Dee. The two usually agreed on most decisions concerning the makeup of Peter's albums, but Dee was not sure that a live album from Peter was justified. Usually live albums are done by groups or performers who have achieved larger success.

Peter felt that his rapport with the audience was so great that a live album would serve him well. "I was communicating with them as much as the music does," Peter says. "They were giving us ovations during songs as well as at the beginning and end. And I said, 'Dee, the next one has gotta be live.' The kids just can't contain themselves at the beginning of a number, and then they go really quiet during an acoustic song. It's great!"

60

So, with a little debate and a little pushing, and a great deal of careful consideration, Dee had to agree with Peter. They listened to tapes of various concerts, and it was only too true. The next album would be a live single album, culled from the best tapes of those outstanding concerts.

After sifting through dozens of tapes over the course of several weeks, Peter was able to narrow his choices down to the versions of several songs which he had selected to be included on the album. Since each time the group did a song in concert it was different, Peter really had his work cut out for him.

"It was originally going to be 'All I Want to Be,' 'Plain Shame,' 'Doobie Wah,' 'Jumping Jack Flash,' 'Lines on My Face,' and 'How Do You Feel.' It added up to a single album. We played it for Jerry Moss, (president of A&M Records) and he turned around and said, 'Where's the rest?'"

"And I said 'What do you mean, more?'"

Actually, this was just what Peter had been after. He had wanted to do a double album all along. Once Jerry Moss and Dee heard just how good the album was, they threw aside all thoughts about the higher price of a double album, of Peter's tenuous "star" status, and of caution. They knew they had a great LP, and they knew the public would agree. What they didn't know, nor even imagine, was just how big it would be.

Peter went back to work in the studio, selecting the rest of the songs, and doing the tedious and exacting job of editing the material down to make it just right for the album. This sort of work is often left to engineers. Most musicians aren't familiar with the intricacies of production, but Peter had always produced his own albums and simply couldn't let anyone do the job for him.

Peter chose the title directly enough, *Frampton Comes Alive!* They put the finishing touches on it and sat back to wait.

The reviews were fantastic, but Peter was too wise to go by the reviews. The success of the album would ultimately depend on one solitary factor: whether people bought it or not.

When an advance copy was sent to WNEW-FM in New York, it got hours and hours of airplay, and fans were calling up to request several of the tunes. Soon, they were calling their record stores demanding to know when they could buy the album.

Within the first month the album was out, it rose steadily up the charts. In one week alone, A & M had to curtail production of other artists' albums in order to meet the Frampton demand. They shipped out one million *Alive!* albums — a record for them. It reached the top ten within that first month. By March, just two months after its release, it was number one. Peter was touring at the time and made sure to thank his fans effusively for their support. He was thrilled and knew, no matter what happened to the album after that, most of his worries were cleared up.

Alive! held that spot for one week and then dropped to number two, as Wings' newest album took over the top position. Peter didn't mind too much; after all, who could expect to compete with a former Beatle? Meanwhile, "Show Me The Way," Peter's favorite from the *Frampton* album, had become the number one single, and he couldn't have been happier. "'Show Me The Way' wasn't even meant to be a single," Peter said. "We put the album out first, then we got the radio playsheets, and that was the track everybody wanted to hear. I'd never had a hit before — no single hits — ever. I'd just been plugging away on tour, just learning," he says in that characteristically modest way.

JFK Stadium, Philadelphia, 1977 *Chuck Pulin*

As the single reached the top, the album went along too. By June *Alive!* was again number one, and everyone was thrilled. It was highly unusual, and, to top it off, *Alive!* remained number one throughout the summer, and well into the fall, for an unprecedented number of weeks. *Alive!* was number one for seventeen weeks, outselling nearly everything else in sight. Now *Frampton Comes Alive!* is the biggest selling double album of all time and continues to sell at a rate that is simply unbelievable.

Everyone from Jerry Moss to Dee to the critics to Peter himself was astonished! Peter was suddenly the hottest rock performer in the nation. He was in demand, and the approval he had been seeking was suddenly his.

Suddenly, Frampton was a *name*. "People don't ask me where I've been, or what I've been doing. They just say, 'Who's he?' as though I dropped out of the sky. Well, I'm the overnight sensation who happened

JFK Stadium, Philadelphia, 1977   *Chuck Pulin*

after more than four years," Peter says with mock exasperation.

All those years of hard knocks, of experiencing the music industry ups and downs, prepared him for his current sweep of the industry. Of course, he never imagined himself being such a star, but he is one man who can handle it, and there is absolutely no trace of personality change in him. He's as sweet and honest, as humble and happy as ever. All his friends attest to this, and even his roadies claim that he's the best star they've ever worked for, that he has handled the whole star thing better than most.

"I'm very, very lucky that I had this much experience — the ten years before this and the five semi pro years before that. That experience of being in bands and around people and learning what not to get hung up on — that's really the thing," Peter says. "The real shame is to see *other* people that you've known for a long time change when *you* haven't."

And it's true. Peter hasn't changed at all. He's more relaxed, more confident, and eminently happier. Also, he has lost none of his vivacity or sincerity. Now that he has paid back all of his debts, he feels more secure and says that his money, after expenses, will be used to make the people around him happy. He's noted for his generosity, and indeed, pays his band members very well, rewarding them with periodic bonuses that are sometimes as high as $75,000. As a gift, Peter gave Dee a 22-karat boxing glove pendant with a diamond in the center. His main concern with money is to pay his bills, to put enough aside in order to live comfortably in the future, and to give others happiness. "But," he says, "the more you have the more of a problem it is. I don't really realize how much (money) there is. I don't phone up every five minutes and say 'How much have we got now?' I don't really want to know. It's a staggering amount, unfortunately." This remark reflects his self-conscious attitude; he is always guarding himself from becoming too cocky. Somehow, it seems impossible that such a thing would ever happen to Peter.

When asked to explain why *Alive!* has become the biggest selling double LP in history, Peter has had to say that he really doesn't know. He attributes some of its success to his constant touring and some to his rapport with the audiences. But he simply cannot account for the record-breaking sales which the album has made. Critics have suggested a variety of reasons. Some say that it is because the album is live and therefore captures Peter's infectious performances which his other albums couldn't do. Others say that it is because the material presented on the album covers a wide range, from mellow-romantic acoustic tunes to hard rocking tunes to some middle of the road numbers. Others have said that Peter's number was simply up; it was his turn to make it. And still others have said that it is because he is so nice and that audiences want a nice hero after all the arrogant ones they've had, that his fifth album was such a dramatic success.

John Rockwell, writing in *The New York Times* (October 3, 1976) suggested that a big reason for *Alive!*'s success was that it is a marked contrast to his "slicker studio efforts." The live album is successful in "capturing a slightly tougher, grittier sound."

Peter feels that the variety of styles he has worked with over the course of his career have helped him in reaching success. The *Alive!* album offers representative tunes from each of these diverse styles and can be seen as a sort of coming together of Peter Frampton's abilities. In any case, the album

JFK Stadium, Philadelphia, 1977 *Chuck Pulin*

has given him an added boost of confidence and the knowledge that he can continue to experiment and grow musically. He is no longer afraid of trying new and unfamiliar styles. That is a tremendous relief for him.

He also offers these possibilities as a tribute to Dee; "Perhaps it's just a combination of keeping the name going, great management, really good handling of my career." It must be a pleasure to work for Peter because he is so very appreciative and always remembers those who help.

The funny thing about *Alive!*'s success is that it made fans aware of his past efforts. After *Alive!* became a "gold record" the *Frampton* album did, too, and people began reaching back into Peter's four previous albums to discover the history of their new star.

65

Madison Square Garden, NYC, 1976   *Chuck Pulin*

Success *has* changed his life, but he has the wonderful capacity to view it from as objective a point of view as possible. "Now it's me being *him* out there," he says. "I could never compete with the LP or with who Peter Frampton is supposed to be. Inside, I'm still marveling at it all from 1000 feet high. It's not me I see."

All the changes in his life strike him as funny. He's surprised when people find him in ordinary places like supermarkets and "someone drops something on the floor right behind me, just because of who I am. Strange," he remarks. Even though his privacy is a little curtailed, he acknowledges that the success and acclaim are worth it. It's the fans he's been courting, so he doesn't mind too much if they want his autograph or to talk for a few minutes, though he does say that he doesn't like to be asked for an autograph when he's eating.

In summing up just how all of this affected him Peter said, "I'll remember this year as like . . . well, it meant relief in a way. But only inasmuch as I can pay my bills. I try not to think about it. I pile up the press clippings and send them off to my mother. She's got a scrapbook going back to when I was about eight. It's just starting to sink in, what's happening. The longer it takes to really sink in, the better."

And sure enough, the first people Peter called when *Alive!* went "gold" were his parents. They were thrilled, and in fact, are thinking of moving to America. In wrapping up a tremendously successful year, Peter looked forward to continuing his demanding tour schedule and to having his parents closer at hand. And, Dee, Peter's adoptive parent, presented him with a classic Rolls Royce Silver Cloud in honor of his success.

It certainly was an amazing year for this young man, and in his own appreciative words, "The album has done the impossible for my career. I'm an extremely happy person. I love this new success, this new life I'm living. And I don't want anything to end it now. I'm ready for more."

HOW PETER COPES
WITH SUCCESS

Peter maintains a steady, easy-going attitude which has helped him to pursue his career with unfailing vigor. As his confidence grew he did not grow cockier, but grew happier. For Peter, confidence simply means that he is relating better with his audience and that they are responding better to him and to his music. Confidence for Peter is an acknowledgment that all he has been working toward was worth the effort. When the audience cheers and supports him, he knows that they are behind him. His feeling that fans feel a part of his hard-won success is true. Peter remains a champion of his audiences, showering them with the love and affection they have so generously given him.

"I'm shaking just talking about it," Peter claims. "It's very emotional . . . but then, people *are* . . . people are buying my life when they're buying those records. I hate to sound bigheaded or something, but that's the reality of it. Suddenly, everything you've been doing means something."

Peter's modesty and sense of reality have certainly been two very large factors which have helped him to maintain his steady sense of self. Dee says that Peter has an amazing capacity for recognizing the pitfalls which he could fall into. "He's seen a lot of groups and artists that I've managed over the years and said, 'Oh my God, that's not going to happen to me.' The minute he seems to feel a situation might be looking even slightly that way, a red light goes on in his head. He just steers away from it. He is a young old man . . ." says Dee, in praise of Peter's judgment.

Peter knows exactly how far to let his new success take him. He has given even more of his immense affection to his fans than before. Rather than putting himself on the pedestal which he has earned, he brings his happiness to the people who have made it all possible for him. More than ever, Peter conscientiously thanks his fans for the kindness they have bestowed on him, easily acknowledging that without them, he wouldn't be where he is now.

Of course, along with the adoration comes a lack of privacy. "I have a lot of people to run interference around me," Peter says. I've never been the center of attention or been known for my jokes, and I'm often suspicious of people's motives in meeting me. They barge right in. Only, the people I'd like to meet — those who respect my privacy — are too intimidated by it all, and I never get to meet them."

Recently, after a few separations, Peter and Penny have broken off their relationship. Whether this is the result of his career or just a clash of their two personalities, Peter is not sure. But it leaves a big gap in his life. With his superstar status, it is extremely difficult for him to meet women now. How can he be sure what their intentions are? How can he know if they are genuine? He doesn't have much time to spend casually meeting people, mainly because his new life doesn't afford him the pleasures of going out anonymously. There are very few places Peter can go for an evening where he won't be recognized and mobbed.

"I can't stand in line for films anymore or go out on the streets alone. There's only one club in Manhattan where I can sit and listen to music and not be hassled."

Happily, he has kept up his friendship with Mary, who now lives in Woodstock, New York, not far from Peter's home. They are close, though he is quick to point out that they will never live together again.

More and more he finds that he likes to stay at home, playing guitar, watching TV, listening to music, walking, and getting together with his close friends; but his life is missing a very important factor: a female companion. He's a homebody who doesn't like one-night-stands. He wants a woman whom he can love and trust and with whom he can share his emotions. Work does seem to get in the way of Peter's relationships, but so many other rock stars have good long-lasting relationships that it seems impossible to believe that Peter won't meet the right woman one of these days.

He's a modest and simple man who loves the plain home life he leads (except, of course, that it lacks a constant love) and who admits that he "lives for the stage." He loves to perform and has said repeatedly that if he didn't love it, he wouldn't be doing it. Certainly, it seems that the major part of his life has been spent on the road, but for Peter, his music is all-important and he believes that appearing in person and giving concerts is what keeps his music fresh and growing. His audiences cover a range of ages, and for Peter it's a pleasure knowing that his music appeals to so many types of people.

"The fans represent a complete spectrum of all age groups," he says. "There are young kids the Top 40 stations are built on — the twelve-year-olds, again, which is really funny for me. But I love it, because they're the ones that made it a hit. And there're the avid Frampton fans who have stuck by me over the years and grew up on The Herd album.

"I feel I must treat each crowd as an individual audience. For that matter, any group of people that comes together to see and hear me perform should expect me to personally relate with them through my work."

For Peter, keeping in contact with his fans is what his success is all about. While his music is highly personal, he knows that his audiences relate to the words as well as the music. He learned his lyric lessons well.

His attitude about success is simply that he shouldn't try to be the man he reads about in the papers, rather, he should keep plugging away doing

Central Park, NYC, 1977 *Chuck Pulin*

what he knows best. He claims that his new acceptance has so exhilarated him that he wants to practice more and more. Rather than feeling tired, he feels more envigorated. Also, he is now able to work toward that professional goal which had been frustrated twice previously. He now knows he can experiment with the several styles he enjoys and swears he won't become locked into any one particular style. Peter's sixth solo album *I'm in You* (a love song to the audience) features some more jazz-oriented music. Instead of feeling trapped by his success, he feels liberated.

This is an important key to understanding why Peter thrives on his music and on live performances. He knows that the next years will be just as hard

JFK Stadium, Philadelphia, 1977   *Chuck Pulin*

as those during which he worked toward this fame. Once an artist has achieved popularity, it's very difficult to maintain it. There is no second-guessing the fans, so the only way to go is forward. And the only motto to believe in is to be true to oneself. Part of Peter's charm and a great deal of his success rests on the fact that he has always stuck to this principle. He may seem a pushover, but he stands firmly for his beliefs. If there is one thing that is certain, it is that Peter Frampton will continue to change and grow musically, to mature and to learn.

For Peter, a large part of remaining true to himself is taking care of himself. His health is extremely important. Because he performs so often,

1976   *Chuck Pulin*

he can't afford to be ill. Touring takes a lot out of an entertainer, but Peter keeps a careful watch on his health while on the road. As a vegetarian, it is especially difficult for him to find enough nourishment while maintaining the hectic pace of touring, but he does because it is of the ultimate importance for him. In his song, "White Sugar," he tells of the problems a vegetarian encounters while traveling.

"It's all a matter of learning how to survive on the road," he says. "I don't party every night. I don't stay up to all hours on the road because when I finally do get off the road from a gig, I usually feel wiped out. I try not to get unhealthy on the road."

Peter is not a smoker and he doesn't take any drugs. In fact, he's never messed with drugs. He says he's seen too many friends lose their happiness and their lives. For Peter, a little wine or beer is enough. It may sound funny to hear that a rock star is not a wild guy. Certainly, that would be the impression of a superstar like Peter, but he prefers to keep his head clear. There are other ways to relax.

"I've always had the ability to sit alone in a room and flake out, not say anything, just completely turn off, whether I'm happy or sad. I guess that's *some* kind of release. I must have given my mother fits because she could never get through to me when I did it as a kid," Peter says.

It's Peter's ability to control his moods, to create his own happiness, and to make his environment comfortable which has helped him to remain sane amidst all the craziness of the music industry. No doubt, this will continue to be a saving factor throughout his life.

Perhaps the biggest thorn in Peter's side is the press' treatment of his personality. Many critics have come down hard on Peter's "niceness." Is it an act? How long can he keep it up? These are the sorts of questions which people throw at Peter, and it's pretty difficult fielding such annoying remarks. Admittedly, it's a rare person today who maintains a "nice" character, who continually comes across as sweet and sincere. Today, there is a tendency to believe that these people are ingenuine. But with Peter, it is not an act. He is what he seems — a simply nice guy. "I'm not gonna apologize for being a nice guy because I can't," Peter says.

Coupled with critics' raised eyebrows at Peter's personality, is a constant finding out that, yes, he really is just that nice. Every critic who writes about Peter Frampton mentions that he is an amazingly sweet person. John Rockwell said this about Peter in *The New York Times*, "Refreshingly, Mr. Frampton is about as pleasant and unaffected a rock star as one is likely to encounter." Even when they pan his music, malign his lyrics, or comment on his clothes, they can't leave out the fact that he has got to be one of the nicest famous men around, if not *the* nicest. And he has even won an award to prove it: Rock Personality of the Year in 1976 from *Billboard* magazine.

Many people think that Peter is a millionaire. That is not quite the truth. He has earned enough money to clear up all of his debts and to buy his New York home and a summer place in the Bahamas. But while these homes may be a bit classier than the average person's, they are not really extravagant. After all, he must live somewhere. Usually, when he needs to relax, to get away from it all, he goes down to the Bahamas. There he finds a sense of peace and can escape the pace which surrounds him. His home

Penny McCall, Peter, Johnny Winter, Edgar Winter, 1977   *Chuck Pulin*

there is a retreat, a vacation home which he has certainly earned. The one true luxury he has given himself is his cabin cruiser which stays docked alongside his Nassau home. When he's in the islands, he finds it an immensely enjoyable pastime.

According to an article in *Time* magazine, Peter had earned $50 million in 1976. Naturally this incensed Peter. First of all, this is a distortion of the truth. That figure represents the money brought in from all the various concerns which marketed Frampton paraphernalia (that included T-shirts, albums, posters, etc.). Most of that money went to the various companies selling those items, not into Peter's pocket. "That $50 million figure was exaggerated," Peter says. "It's not the truth at all. That $50 million includes all the money made by a lot of people, including me. But when folks see that figure they start thinking that's what I've got myself . . . in my pocket, that I can pull it out and say, 'Oh yes, here's a mil right here.'"

Naturally no wealthy person wants his income, whether real or exaggerated, publicized. It makes him a target for any number of crimes.

We have only to look through the newspapers for the past few years, to see just how many kidnappings, robberies, and assaults have been committed against known wealthy citizens. This is another reason why Peter prefers to live modestly and to remain uncontroversial. You will notice that his comings and goings, outside of concert appearances, are not highly publicized. He is not a flashy personality like many of his rock contemporaries. And, as much as he prefers his life this way, it is a precaution against losing whatever privacy he has left.

As 1976, the most exciting year in Peter's life, was drawing to a close, he looked back on everything that happened to him with awe, wonder, and

JFK Stadium, Philadelphia, 1977   *Chuck Pulin*

supreme happiness. But he couldn't totally relax — he was busy thinking about his next album. It would have to be big to follow *Alive!*, the biggest selling double album of all time. Long before he even went into the studio to work on the new album, he had most of the songs composed. There were lots of bits and pieces he had been jotting down for future use, and now he would have the chance to put them to work for him. His next album would be a bit more experimental. He could do that now. He had the confidence that he could intertwine all sorts of material to make this next LP really different.

But first a little vacation. Peter went to his New York home to relax, but found that he couldn't. So, he took a few close friends and went off to the Bahamas. There he found it a bit easier to let all the tension ebb from him; but, still, he was pondering over the next LP. He was excited about it. He wanted it to be even better than *Alive!* Naturally, he couldn't expect it to sell as phenomenally as *Alive!*, but he wanted it to take off from the *Frampton* album, which he considers his best studio LP.

Peter is always jotting down ideas, bits and pieces of lyrics for songs, and taping various ideas for tunes. "When it comes time to do an album," he says, "I get all the cassettes out, play them all, as well as some new stuff, put them together, and make a song. It's a lot like when everybody had homework from college; you might have a whole vacation to do it, but you do it two nights before or the night before. Well, that's the way I do it, only I'm making notes all the time. I've got it all filed and I just bring it out and the first couple of days I just sit around and listen to all that I've written over the last few months."

He makes it sound so simple, but actually the whole process is totally engrossing. Peter can't write on the road, and, since so much of his time is spent touring, he must hole up at home with his material spread around him and devote himself entirely to composing. "I prefer to be next to a piano with peace and quiet," he says.

In this fashion, Peter set about to work on his sixth album. He had plenty of ideas for it and had originally wanted to record it in the same Motown Studios in Detroit where Stevie Wonder recorded his early hits. Before he had the chance to ask Motown, word leaked out through a magazine, who called up Motown to confirm whether or not it was true. Motown told the magazine that it was not, and Peter was thwarted. "I never got a chance to ask, myself," he said. "I felt bad about that."

With this problem settled for him, Peter still wanted his long-time idol, Stevie Wonder, to play harmonica on the LP but was too timid to ask. They had met for the first time on a television award show and Peter was so very excited that his knees were actually shaking. But it was Peter's mother who was instrumental in really getting Stevie to agree. Mr. and Mrs. Frampton were visiting Peter, and Mrs. Frampton asked Peter if he was going to ask Stevie to play on his next album. He said he didn't know, and his mother pushed, telling him that it couldn't hurt to ask. Sure enough, she was right. Stevie said he'd be glad to play on one of his albums, anytime.

It seemed that, one by one, all of Peter's remotest dreams were coming true. What else could happen? While recording the tune "Rocky Hot Club" (which Peter describes as "very disco oriented") on which Stevie played

Penny McCall, 1977   *Chuck Pulin*

harmonica, it turned out that Mick Jagger was recording in the next studio. He came over and lent a hand to Peter's record. You'll hear Jagger's voice along with Peter's on the background vocals of "Tried to Love." The title song, "I'm in You" was written about Peter and the audience. He swears he wrote it without any sexual implications and that he was thinking on a spiritual level about his tremendous love for and rapport with his audiences. The fans love it, and Peter's efforts found nearly as much support as his last work had.

I'm in You was no disappointment to the fans who anxiously awaited Peter's newest release. In fact, orders piled in way before the album was ever shipped to the record stores. There were enough advance orders for

I'm in You to qualify it immediately for "gold record" status, thus insuring Peter's place among the greats.

There was a seven month interim between the last tour for his *Alive!* album, and the first tour for his *I'm in You* album. Peter was afraid that such a long layoff would hurt his performance. He was extremely nervous for that next tour, even more nervous than he usually is. "I don't quite get to the point of throwing up before the first concert of a tour, I become very, very quiet." He was so thoroughly worried, though, about how the fans would react to him after so long, that afterwards he said, "I feel like I've just been to the dentist. I feel alleviated of a ton of pressure. It's nice to know they're still there after seven months." Though they loved him every bit as much as they had before, he said that he would never take that much time off again. "I'm still learning, and today was another great lesson. What I learned today was not to take seven months off again. I love to feel well-oiled. I didn't feel that way today, but the audience helped me." On stage, Peter turned around to see his parents and Mary backstage cheering him on, while out in the audience approximately 90,000 people crowded into JFK Stadium in Philadelphia to welcome him. This certainly was a testament to the amazing appeal of Peter's work.

SGT. PEPPER

Peter's next venture, *Sgt. Pepper's Lonely Hearts Club Band*, was a departure from his normal routine — but not so far as may be imagined. *Sgt. Pepper* is a movie dedicated to the joy of music. In this extravaganza, Peter plays Billy Shears, the young and phenomenally talented guitarist who strikes out for fame as a rock musician. From these few sentences alone, it is apparent that Peter is not too far from the story himself. In fact, he doesn't have a single speaking line; he sings. For these reasons, both Dee and Peter decided that *Sgt. Pepper* would be the right vehicle for Peter to break into films. Dee was executive producer of the movie.

"I felt that it wasn't a tremendous acting challenge for him," Dee said. "His roots are the Beatles and you're not taking him out of his own environment. You're not saying, 'Hey he's become a superstar, now he's going out and making a movie.' I think the timing and the luck fall in, too, that this kind of vehicle came along at the perfect time."

Both men wanted it clearly understood that Peter wasn't trying to cash in on his star status by attempting an acting career. Rather, the role came along. It was perfect for Peter. It was Peter, and he is Billy Shears — an honest, sweet and eminently talented young musician. "He's playing himself," adds Dee. "A rock star singing songs of a group he idolized and grew up with. What a great opportunity!"

"I don't think the lads will be displeased with what we're doing to their music," says Peter. Actually the movie uses songs from many of the Beatles albums, including the score from the immortal *Sgt. Pepper* LP. Peter sings "Golden Slumbers" and "The Long and Winding Road," two lovely soothing numbers perfectly suited to his ethereal image and softer side; and "She Came in Through the Bathroom Window," a more rollicking and robust tune, is done with the Bee Gees, Peter's "Sgt. Pepper's Band." The group does a variety of Beatles tunes, including "With a Little Help from My Friends," to "Getting Better."

All together, making the movie was a world of fun, and Peter soon overcame any shyness he felt in front of the camera. After a short time, he said that he felt no distraction and really enjoyed working in this new

1976   *Chuck Pulin*   Frampton's Camel

medium. Actually, a few years before, Peter had a cameo spot in a little known movie with Ringo Starr called *Countdown,* but the work for that was nothing on the scale of his involvement with *Sgt. Pepper.* He had to give up six months of touring to work on the movie, but he enjoyed every minute of it. Along with his own part, he was thrilled to meet the well-known actors and musicians who had roles, large and small, in the movie.

George Burns, the veteran radio, television, motion picture and night club performer, played the lovable mayor of Heartland, Mr. Kite. Dressed in white, he cavorts with the satin-suited Sgt. Pepper's band and joins them to sing "For the Benefit of Mr. Kite."

The Bee Gees (Barry, Robin, and Maurice Gibb) have come full circle in their amazing fifteen-year rock career. Their hits range from the innovative tunes they popularized in the 60's ("I've Got to Get a Message to You," and "I Started a Joke") to the slick disco sounds they are now noted for in such songs as "You Should Be Dancing," and their *Saturday Night Fever* hits. The three play Mark, Dave, and Bob Henderson, respectively, the three members of Billy Shears' band.

A number of well-known musicians, singers, and personalities played smaller parts. Among them was the comedian who has taken the world by storm, Steve Martin, who only has to smile to make you laugh. Martin plays the diabolical Dr. Maxwell Edison, and he plays it to the hilt, singing "Maxwell's Silver Hammer."

Several guest stars included Aerosmith and Earth, Wind & Fire and two giants, Alice Cooper and Billy Preston, who plays the role of Sgt. Pepper. It was certainly a thrill for Peter to work with all these performers and, in many cases, meeting them for the first time. "People don't realize that we have our idols, too," he later said.

Before Peter was chosen for the role of Billy Shears, producer Robert Stigwood was contemplating using John Denver. He might have been a good choice, but could he have brought the vigor and exuberance which Peter did to the role? Still riding high on the walloping successes of *Saturday Night Fever* and *Grease,* Robert Stigwood, every bit of a perfectionist as Peter, caught wind of Peter's ascendance among the greats. He realized what a vibrant and happy guy Peter is and knew that the role was made for him. In fact, Peter's looks and personality match exactly the character that scriptwriter Henry Edwards had called for, "a young and handsome guitar player."

Because Stigwood is noted for his perfectionism and, incidentally, for the success of his ventures, Dee and Peter felt that they couldn't go wrong working with him. After reading the script, they saw nothing offensive, just a

Penny McCall, Rock Music Awards, 1976   *Frank Edwards/Fotos International*

fun, pleasant tribute to the music of a musical institution: The Beatles.

To film the grand finale scene (where the mayor, the Band, and all the townspeople of Heartland gather in a wild parade in front of Heartland City Hall to sing the theme song) producer Stigwood arranged an unparalleled bash.

He began by sending out engraved invitations all over the world to over one hundred of the most famous people in music. Those accepting were jetted into Hollywood, given rooms at the famed Beverly Wilshire Hotel, and provided with private limousine service for the duration of their stay. Each guest was presented with two gifts: a solid gold Sgt. Pepper's medallion and a director's chair with his or her name appliqued in silk.

When the guests arrived, they assembled on the set in bleachers behind Peter and the Bee Gees, making a replica of the extraordinary photo-montage cover from the Beatle's album and began their version of the title tune.

Among the celebrities present were: Peter Allen, Keith Allison, Stephen Bishop, George Benson, Elvin Bishop, Jack Bruce, Keith Carradine, Jim Seals and Dash Crofts, Jim Dandy, Yvonne Elliman, Jose Feliciano, Dr. John, Nils Lofgren, Mark Lindsay, John Mayall, Curtis Mayfield, and

"Cousin Brucie" Morrow; not to mention Peter Noone (Herman of Herman's Hermits), Robert Palmer, Bonnie Raitt, Helen Reddy, Minnie Ripperton, Johnny Rivers, Al Stewart, Stephen Stills, Tina Turner, Johnny Winter, Bob Weir, and Hank Williams, Jr., and the groups Heart and Sha Na Na. All sang and danced up a storm and then were released from the "work" to indulge in a twelve-hour party, all at the expense of Stigwood. Tables bedecked with gourmet delicacies from champagne and oysters to filet mignon and prime ribs, strolling violinists, and a dance floor made for one wild party. It was a fest where eighty-two-year-old George Burns and twenty-nine-year-old Peter Frampton could be found dancing side by side — a party in the true spirit of Heartland. When it was all over, Robert Stigwood, who signed the $500,000 check said that it was a "night of joy and entertainment. It was worth every penny. A perfect finale to a wonderful movie."

As a memento of the filming and party, the guests signed two autograph books; one to be kept by RSO Films and the other to be auctioned off, with the proceeds going to the National Multiple Sclerosis Society.

Sandy Farina, Sgt. Pepper's *UPI*

TODAY & FUTURE

It should be obvious enough that Peter Frampton intends to keep right on doing just what he is doing now. No one could love touring more than he. Peter claims that the road is as exciting as it is exhausting. "I think I've proved that it must be exciting or I wouldn't have spent this much time on the road in the last two or three years," he explains. He enjoys it and he knows its importance in keeping in touch with his audience. In the liner notes for his *Alive!* album, Peter underscores exactly how he feels about touring. "Performing is the best thing for a musician. It keeps my music alive and breathing; that's too important to give up. I really don't think I'll ever stay off the road for very long."

Along with his constant touring, Peter says that his new popularity has made him go back home and practice more than ever before. When a tour is finished, he relaxes only long enough to find the strength to practice again. He is a man of boundless energy, especially when it comes to his only true love — his music. And there are other artists Peter enjoys listening to as well. Today his tastes run to his melodic contemporaries, Jackson Browne and Stevie Wonder, as well as his more jazz flavored favorites, Little Feat and the immortal Django Reinhart. Peter claims to own "umpteen thousands" of Django albums.

Best of all for Peter, his new fame has given him that added confidence which always seemed lacking. He is still shy, and all those sheltered years remain with him; but, on stage and off, he has an added self-assurance. "I'm more self-confident socially. I never went out when I lived at home, never rode the motor bikes, never had friends my own age, because from eight to sixteen I always lived with my guitar. You see, I didn't *go* to parties, I *played* them," Peter says, by way of explaining his social manners. Peter also says that he has always been shy, citing that "socially, I'll stand in a corner and shake." He says that he's never been the type to command attention in a crowd and is often uncomfortable when he's introduced to people. He prefers to mingle in crowds, meeting people on his own terms. He says that he enjoys being a celebrity now, and has learned, through all of his experiences, how to best cope with individuals as well as groups.

Donna Summer Billboard #1 Music Awards, 1977 *UPI*

Peter's confidence grew gradually. With each successive concert, with each show of greater appreciation from fans, his stage presence matured and so did his personality. Now, he feels confident as a performer, as a singer, a writer, and as a man. He feels uncomfortable when he senses that people are nervous meeting him, but he can thoroughly understand that situation. Peter remembers meeting George Harrison once and being so nervous that he couldn't think of what to say. "I came out with something so inane that I thought I was an idiot. But I was imagining the whole thing."

With all of his own experiences in mind, Peter can go ahead understanding both sides of the coin. These days he finds meeting people and being in social situations very easy to cope with. It's a part of life which had to come later for him, because he spent so much time during his youth outside of the normal growing patterns.

"I'm not worried now about trying something that's a little off-the-wall," Peter says. "You have to believe in yourself. I'm in a position now where I'm doing exactly what I want to do on stage, and people like it. I'm very lucky. But then, it's my third time around. Now, I know exactly what I want to do."

Sometime in the near future Peter plans to try using brass sections and some strings with his live act, in order to add a new dimension and to further experiment with his music. Whatever he does, we can rest assured that Peter Frampton will continue to grow and offer his fans the finest in rock music.

He also would like to produce albums for other performers. His expertise as a producer, which he has ably demonstrated on all of his own albums, has brought him to the attention of several artists who would like to make use of his engineering talents.

JFK Stadium, Philadelphia, 1977   *Chuck Pulin*

Jerry Shirley, 1977   *Chuck Pulin*

A secret dream of Peter's is to write the score for a movie and to appear in it. He'd like to do all the music and have someone write a script. When he explains the type of film he'd like to work with, Peter puts it this way: "I like the movies that make me cry. I'd like to be in a crying movie." A simple and romantic explanation, and, frankly, it would be easy to imagine him in a role of this sort.

But Peter is wise and wants his entire life to fall in place. Although he readily admits his devotion to music is totally absorbing, he certainly knows that it takes more than song to make his life complete. "I don't want my career to eat all my senses away," he says. "I've got to find someone to love and care about." This remark is so characteristic of Peter. While others might say they need someone to love them and to care about them, Peter instinctively goes deeper. He knows that for him to be a whole person, he needs to love someone as much as he needs to be loved. Yet again, as is typical of him, he can look to the bright side of his life and point it out with pride. "Things have been going well," he says. "I feel elated at the response I have been getting around the country. I have much to rejoice about and my work mirrors that."

Looking back over Peter Frampton's extraordinary career, glimpsing with infallible hindsight at the bumps and curves along his way, we see an amazingly driven man. We see a man who grew from boyhood through youth and into manhood completely dedicated to finding truth for himself in music. We can only admire such a devoted artist and wish him all the best.

John Belushi, Meadowlands Stadium, NJ, 1978   *Chuck Pulin*
Leif Garrett, John Belushi   *Chuck Pullin*

John Belushi, Meadowlands Stadium, NJ, 1978   *Chuck Pulin*

Sgt. Pepper's   *Judi Lesta*

DISCOGRAPHY

LOOKING THRU YOU (1968) The Herd, Fontana Records

AS SAFE AS YESTERDAY (1969) Humble Pie, Andrew Oldham's
    Immediate Label

Desperation	I'll Go Alone
Stick Shift	Bang
Buttermilk Boy	Alabama '69
Growing Closer	Nifty Little Number Like You
As Safe As Yesterday	What You Will

TOWN AND COUNTRY (1969) Humble Pie, Andrew Oldham's
    Immediate Label

Take Me Back	Ollie, Ollie
Sad Bag Of Shaky Jake	Heartbeat
Light Of Love	Only You Can Say
Cold Lady	Silver Tongue
Down Home Again	Home And Away
Every Mother's Son	

HUMBLE PIE (1970) A & M 4270

Live With Me	Theme From Skint — See
Only A Roach	You Later Liquidator
Earth And Water Song	Red Light Mama
One Eyed Trouser-Snake Rumba	Red Hot
I'm Ready	Sucking On The Sweet Vine

ROCK ON (1971) Humble Pie, A & M 4301

Shine On	Song For Jenny
Sour Grain	Light
79th And Sunset	Big George
Stone Cold Fever	Strange Days
Rolling Stone	Red Neck Jump

ROCKIN' THE FILLMORE — PERFORMANCE (1972) Humble Pie,
    A & M 3306

Four Day Creep	
I'm Ready	Rolling Stone
Stone Cold Fever	Hallelujah
I Walk On Gilded Splinters	I Don't Need No Doctor

LOST AND FOUND (1972) Humble Pie, A & M 3513

WIND OF CHANGE (1972) Peter Frampton, A & M 4348

Fig Tree Bay	Oh For Another Day
Wind of Change	All I Want To Be (Is By Your Side)
Lady Lieright	The Lodger
Jumping Jack Flash	Hard
It's A Plain Shame	Alright

FRAMPTON'S CAMEL (1973) Peter Frampton, A & M 4389

I've Got My Eyes On You	White Sugar
All Night Long	Don't Fade Away
Lines On My Face	Just The Time Of Year
Which Way The Wind Blows	Do You Feel Like We Do
I Believe (When I Fall in Love with You it will be Forever)	

SOMETHIN'S HAPPENING (1974) A & M 3619

Doobie Wah	Baby (Somethin's Happening)
Golden Goose	Waterfall
Underhand	Magic Moon
I Wanna Go To The Sun	Sail Away

FRAMPTON (1975) A & M 4512

Day's Dawning	Nassau
Show Me The Way	Baby I Love Your Way
One More Time	Apple Of Your Eye
The Crying Clown	Penny For Your Thoughts
Fanfare	Money
Nowhere's Too Far	

FRAMPTON COMES ALIVE! (1976) A & M 3703

Introduction	
Somethin's Happening	I Wanna Go To The Sun
Doobie Wah	Penny For Your Thoughts
Show Me The Way	(I'll Give You) Money
It's A Plain Shame	Shine On
All I Want To Be (Is By Your Side)	Jumping Jack Flash
Wind Of Change	Lines On My Face
Baby I Love Your Way	Do You Feel Like We Do

I'M IN YOU (1977) A & M 4704
I'm In You
(Puttin' My) Heart On The Line
St. Thomas (Don't You Know How I Feel)
Won't You Be My Friend
Signed, Sealed, Delivered (I'm Yours)

You Don't Have To Worry
Tried To Love
Rocky's Hot Club
(I'm A) Road Runner

SINGLES DISCOGRAPHY

From The Underworld (1968) The Herd, Fontana Records
Natural Born Boogie (1969) Humble Pie, Andrew Oldham's Immediate
 Label
Show Me The Way (1976) Peter Frampton, A & M
Do You Feel Like We Do (1976) Peter Frampton, A & M
I'm In You (1977) Peter Frampton, A & M
Tried To Love (1977) Peter Frampton, A & M

AWARDS

1976 "Rock Personality of the Year," *Billboard* Magazine
1977 "Artist of the Year," Rock Music Awards
1977 "Top Recording Artist of the Year," *Rolling Stone* Magazine